PRAISE THE PIG

PRAISE THE PIG

Loin to Belly, Shoulder to Ham—
Pork-Inspired Recipes for Every Meal

JENNIFER L. S. PEARSALL

SKYHORSE PUBLISHING

Skyhorse Publishing books may be purchased in bulk at special discounts for sales promotion, corporate gifts, fund-raising, or educational purposes. Special editions can also be created to specifications. For details, contact the Special Sales Department, Skyhorse Publishing, 307 West 36th Street, 11th Floor, New York, NY 10018 or info@skyhorsepublishing.com.

Skyhorse® and Skyhorse Publishing® are registered trademarks of Skyhorse Publishing, Inc.®, a Delaware corporation.

Visit our website at www.skyhorsepublishing.com.

10 9 8 7 6 5 4 3 2 1

Library of Congress Cataloging-in-Publication Data is available on file.

Cover design by Rain Saukas

Print ISBN: 978-1-63450-435-5
Ebook ISBN: 978-1-5107-0039-0

Printed in China

TABLE OF CONTENTS

CHAPTER 3—PORK SAUSAGE AND GROUND PORK 111

INTRODUCTION

Without a doubt, *Praise the Pig* grew out of my first book, *The Big Book of Bacon* (Skyhorse Publishing). That first book started as a joke. Someone in my social media circles asked for advice on cooking a snow goose, a bird that can sometimes be less than a culinary delight. Of course, that sometimes means that other times it's grand, but if you don't cook a bird like that on a regular basis, it can be a challenge to get it right.

Now, I'd cooked snow goose to rounds of applause before and, so, offered up my recipe to the comment stream, ending with, "Be sure to cover the birds with bacon." For some reason, that struck a chord with people. Soon, the words "just add bacon" were being advised for everything from poached pears to pancakes to fixing whatever is wrong with your spouse. People plastered my Facebook wall with the meme "Bacon is the duct tape of the kitchen"; bacon, it seemed, was a cure-all for everything.

So that's how the first book started and, well, this second one just seemed a natural route to take from there. I actually intended to be a little avant-garde, if you will, with this one. I thought about pâtés and headcheeses and things that used cheeks and feet and hocks and tails. But the more I thought about it and the more reading I did into recipe origins that used such parts, I realized that they just weren't *accessible*. I don't mean just the porcine parts themselves, but also the recipes and the tools required to arrive at the tender delicacies that are the art of *charcuterie*. While I love experimenting with food off the beaten path, I think I'm wise enough to know that such a thing isn't everyone's cup of tea. So, where did that leave this book?

"Accessible" really is the key here. I'm not just talking about the ingredients, though some will be harder to find than others, just as is the case with any cookbook that doesn't start each recipe with a can of Campbell's Cream of Mushroom Soup. When I think about "accessible" and cooking, I'm really thinking that the user has to look at the recipe title, glance over the list of ingredients and think, "Yea, I think that would be cool to make and I can pull that off."

Let's face it, dealing with a whole pig's head is intimidating to most of us, me included. Someday I'll tackle that—like when I have a stove and a pot big enough to accommodate such an "ingredient"—but that and cheeks and tongues and tails and the entire art of *charcuterie* are things best designated as specialties, and I didn't think they were right for this book.

That brings me to what this book *is* then. Well, it's a couple things.

Many of the recipes I worked up simply by substituting pork for another meat. One of my favorites, for instance, is the wild rice stew I normally make with roast chicken, but this time made instead with roast pork loin shaved thin—and it ended up being delightful. Pork substitution is especially worthy when it comes to ground beef. Now, I love beef. Give me a good steak or a juicy hamburger any day of the week and I'm a very happy girl. But when it comes to things like chilies and Bolognese sauces, I slowly transitioned from half beef and half pork to all ground pork. I find the results to be more succulent, the bite between the teeth more tender, the overall flavor profile richer. These are the things you discover when you work on a single-subject cookbook.

If simply substituting pork for beef or chicken were all it took, this book would have been far easier. As it turned out, the more I worked with pork, the more inventive I became with it. Recipes like pork with butternut squash, snow peas, and mushrooms in a tarragon cream sauce is one such example, the tasso and red lentil stew another among many.

Lots of these recipes use meat leftover from a bigger roast, most notably the ham and the shoulder or Boston butt. A big part of the reason for this is because I live by myself and have to think up things to do with the leftovers from these big cuts. For instance, I spend a lot of the spring, summer, and early fall months smoking Boston butts, because I love a good pulled pork sandwich almost as much as I like getting kissed by a handsome guy, maybe more. But after three days of sandwiches, I'm still faced with the need to do something else with pounds of smoked pork. Same goes for ham—there's only so many ham sandwiches one can eat so many days in a row. So, as you wander these pages, realize that many recipes came from these bigger cuts. I think this "in-depth" use of leftovers, for one, gives you a good excuse to cook shoulders and hams outside of once-a-year summer family reunions and Easter. More importantly, though, it provides options, lets your creativity flow, and gets you out of the tenderloin and pork chop route that's easy to fall into because these smaller cuts are so much more, well, manageable.

Sausage is another bit of porky goodness that dominates in this book. You'll find some specialties, like Portuguese chourico and a custom fennel seed and black pepper blend my local butcher makes. Like other more obscure ingredients such as tasso and the like, I'm fully aware that you may not have ready access to such treats. However, I've tried like the dickens to give you a resource if I had one, both a taste and flavor profile for the chosen meat, and a recommendation for a variant and spices that would closely mimic what I've used.

It's that creativity that's really the point. I'm not a professional cook. I've not spent long hours under the tutelage of Mario Batali, I'm not on the board of the James Beard Foundation, and I've never been on *Chopped* or *Knife Fight* or *Iron Chef*. (On the other hand, I'm also far, far away from being nominated as a contestant on *Worst Cooks in America*, so there's that). What I am is a pretty talented home cook who has a good sense for what goes together. I'm also not afraid to step out of bounds, take the foundations of another recipe (or even three), and make it my own.

If I had a hope for this book, it's that you'd do the same. Don't have an ingredient I listed or don't like one of the components? Switch it out to something that works for you. Yes, in more than a few recipes I've stressed where a technique or ingredient shouldn't be changed, as they are essential to making the finished product what it was intended to be. But nobody's holding your fingers to the blue flame of your gas stove. Do what you need to in order to make these recipes work for *you*. Too much cayenne? Substitute it with a little bit of black pepper. I like my meatloaf with extra egg in it, usually one more than most recipes call for. You may not like it that way, and that's okay, skipping the extra won't cost you a thing. None of this book is that hard.

Speaking of hard, lots of cookbooks provide you with a difficulty rating. I don't think any of what you'll read here will make you faint from a lack of confidence. You should have the basics down of hard-boiling an egg, making toast and a sandwich, and roasting your basic chicken. Beyond that I will walk you through how I did certain things, which may not be *le Cordon Bleu*-approved, but that worked in my meager kitchen. If I tell you to fold something a certain way or whisk something constantly, it's because any other way and I would have pulled all my hair out. But this, too, is like the ingredients: If you have a way that works better for you, have at it. Nobody is standing over your shoulder criticizing the uniformity of your carrot chop or your egg white whipping skills.

I hope you have fun with this book and I hope it inspires you to have fun with pork. Pigs are wonderful animals that offer up a cornucopia of mouthwatering fare, so give chicken and beef a time out and Praise the Pig.

—Jennifer L. S. Pearsall

A—Cheeks/Jowls
B—Shoulder/Boston butt cut
C—Shoulder/Picnic roast
D—Loin/Tenderloin/Ribs

E—Belly/Pork belly (which becomes bacon)
F—Ham
G—Hocks

NOTES ABOUT THIS BOOK

BUTCHERS

If you can find a private butcher who handles pig butchering on a regular basis, start experimenting with what they have, especially in the way of sausages and smoked meats. My butcher here in Connecticut has a really nice variety of sausages they stuff in house. Discovering his fennel and black pepper sausage, for instance, was a stroke of luck and helped counter the dearth of chicken and turkey sausages my rather health-conscious grocery store tends to stock. I don't like everything he makes—his chorizo is mild and doesn't hold its bright orange color when cooked—but at least I have options the grocery store doesn't provide.

So what do you do if you don't have a butcher local enough (or budget-friendly enough) to work with? Well, mail order is always a route. A specialty brand of gourmet products I use is D'Artagnan. This company has high-quality and often hard to find sausages, pâtés, and the like and they will FedEx your order overnight. A few minutes of Googling will turn up similar options.

COOKING TEMPERATURES AND THE MODERN PIG

Today's pork isn't what it used to be—it's better. As I write this book, I am on the cusp of turning fifty. That means I grew up in a world of tough, dry pork chops that had nothing to do with my mother's otherwise admirable skills in the kitchen and everything to do with the fear of the day, way back when—the dreaded food-borne parasite known as the *Trichinella spiralis* roundworm.

Sounds pretty icky, eh? Well, it is (or at least from today's standpoint, mostly was). *Trichinella* roundworm larval cysts in raw meat that survived a cooking would then go on to exact its revenge on your digestive system. According to the website medicinenet.com, the gastric acid and pepsin in your stomach work like fairy dust to release the roundworm larvae from their cyst casings. The baby worms take up residence in your small bowel, where they quickly enter their raucous teenage years and party-all-the-time twenties of adulthood. Being the host of such a frat house comes with a price, of course: cramps, nausea, diarrhea, fever, and vomiting at first. After a week, the sorority sisters are beer-bonging as steadily as the guy worms, and you know what happens then. That's right—they release larvae, which float away to make a nursery in your muscles. This brings on the secondary phase of symptoms, more of the first set, plus itching, muscle aches, joint aches, chills, hemorrhaging under the fingernails (e-gads!), and conjunctivitis of the eyes. Pretty miserable stuff, and while the symptoms will go away on their own for most people, a handful will develop extreme secondary issues and die.

That, thank goodness, was the pig of the mid-twentieth century. In 1980, according to a Wikipedia page on the subject, the US government implemented the Federal Swine Protection Act, which, among other things, disallowed feeding garbage to pigs and implemented what would seem to be common-sense policies, such as improved rodent control on hog farms.

Say what you want about the shape of the US government today, the Federal Swine Protection Act was likely one of its smarter moves. Today's mass-produced hogs are likely healthier, if not happier (and no, I don't want to engage in a conversation on breeding crates or overcrowded hog barns or slaughter practices, so just leave it alone), than they were back when I was a kid. The good news is that, with the virtual eradication of *Trichinella* in commercially available pork products—an infection or three do surface each year, mostly from small, independent pork producers, but also from wild pigs and the occasional undercooked boar roast a few hunters will consume—we no longer have to cook our pork in a manner better befitting a crematorium.

This confirmation that a lower internal cooking temperature is safe is most beneficial to the very lean cuts, like pork loins, tenderloins, and chops. The normal finished internal temperature used to be in the 160- to 170-degree range back when I was a kid in the 1960s and '70s. Today, thanks to a 2011 edict by the US Department of Agriculture, most whole meat cuts will be just fine and dandy when an internal temperature of 145 degrees is reached and maintained for a bit. This means that if you're using older cookbooks, like those from Julia Child or the iconic *Joy of Cooking*, reduce your temperatures and likely your cooking times.

If you're not sure about the doneness of your pork, go right ahead and use a probe thermometer inserted into the deepest part of your cut of meat, though not up against any bone that may be present. When you're close to that magic 145 degrees, take your meat from the heat, cover it with foil and let it rest, a few minutes for something like medium-thick pork chops, maybe seven to ten minutes for a good-size tenderloin, twenty minutes for a thick loin roast (a very lean cut), and even a half-hour for a full crown roast. During that resting time, the temperature will continue to rise. That rest also lets the juices, which have retreated from the heat of the oven or grill to gather in the deepest part of your cut, to rise back to the surface and provide that uniformly juicy bite when you do stick a fork in it.

There are three exceptions to this new temperature "rule." Both uncured pork belly, which generally takes a slow cook to perfect, and ground pork are better cooked to higher temperatures. No, you cannot and should not order an all-pork burger cooked only to rare. Get your all-pork burger to just under medium and don't worry about it drying out; an 80/20 (80-percent meat, 20-percent fat) mix of pork, I firmly believe, stays moister than the same meat-to-fat ratio of ground beef. Don't believe me? Cook a beef burger and a ground pork burger side by side to medium and give them the ol' taste test. I guarantee the pork burger will be juicier with the possible exception of an exceptionally high-quality grind of beef, such as that of the organic grass-fed variety. The third piece of pork that should be cooked to a higher temperature is the pork shoulder, also known as the Boston butt and picnic in its top and bottom halves, respectively.

DEALING WITH THE BIG BOY—PORK SHOULDERS (BOSTON BUTTS AND PICNICS)

The pork shoulder portions or Boston butts I've used for many of the recipes here have been prepared in a variety of ways. Pork shoulder actually comes in two cuts, and it's worth knowing the difference between the two.

The top and front-most part of the pig's shoulder is called either simply a pork shoulder or, depending on where you live, a Boston butt. They are the same piece of meat and you will find them available both bone-in and boneless. The bottom part of the shoulder is called a "picnic." It is a smaller cut and one leaner than the Boston butt cut, but it is also usually a bit cheaper by at least a couple dollars a pound. Aside from the picnic not having quite the same fatty content as the upper shoulder part, thus requiring shorter cooking times, the biggest problem I've seen is that they're just not available everywhere. Southern states, those below the Mason Dixon line, generally have grocery stores that stock them, while grocery store attendants where I lived in Wisconsin looked at me like I had three heads when I asked for one.

If I have a choice, and especially if I'm looking to use one of these cuts to develop several other recipes, I'll go with the Boston butt every time. I also always look for this cut (as well as that of the picnic) bone-in, since the bone imparts a richness to the finished flavor, a flavor that is worth the inconvenience of the longer cooking times bone-in cuts require. Anyhow, the Boston butt's succulence is undeniable and I think that, with a little care, it's hard to screw up its cooking. The bigger cut is also good for feeding a crowd, though the same could be said for using an entire shoulder, which, of course, is the Boston butt and picnic cuts still in their original one-piece arrangement. The picnic, by the way, is what I'll use when I don't have a lot of time on my hand to play with the smoker (or if I've gotten a late start in the day with a recipe build), and yet still have a hankering for a pulled pork sandwich. I believe all the recipes in this book that featured a pork shoulder used the Boston butt cut, so what follows will be germane to that.

I've cooked Boston butts in the slow cooker, slow-roasted them in a lower-temperature oven, and smoked them. I rarely use a probe thermometer to tell if one of my shoulders is finished, because, frankly, when mine are done, the meat falls off the bone. If you prefer yours less cooked than that, want one a little firmer in finished texture to allow for slicing rather than shredding, or if you just haven't played with a large piece of meat like this to be comfortable calling it done without a probe temperature reading, well, then go ahead. A finished roast should read somewhere in the 190-degree range with the probe inserted in the thickest part of the meat (but not touching the bone on a bone-in cut). Is this higher than it needs to be for health considerations, such as the killing off of the now almost non-existent *Thrichinella* roundworm and the real concern of salmonella? Yes, it is. But this internal 190 degrees should have been arrived at very slowly, because that's what it takes to break down the heavy fat and the tough muscle, and to change the texture of the collagen in the meat to gelatin, which makes a perfectly done shoulder roast succulent rather than chewy. I cannot emphasize the slow aspect of this cooking process for this particular cut enough: Shoot your internal temp to 190 degrees fast and you'll end up with a dry, chewy, overcooked platter of meat only the dog will likely want. Think a moss-covered chunk of almost-set cement. Blech.

Okay, now that we've cleared up that little matter, let's get on to getting this beast of a meat hunk cooked, shall we?

SLOW COOKER

By far the easiest method, this yields the least flavorful shoulder, but, at the same time, one of the most tender. Why? A good pork shoulder or Boston butt should have a good fat cap on one side of it—I'm not talking anything like the couple inches you'd find with pork belly, but maybe a quarter- to half-inch deep on some. Between that glorious protective layer of pretty white fat and the fat within the muscle itself, this cut renders out a lot of liquid fat in the slow cooker. In fact, the roast will be in a bath of rendered fat when you're done cooking it; my average nine-pound Boston butt will go for eight to nine hours in my slow cooker set to the low setting. This will have removed and dissolved to near flavorless-ness any rub you'd have done to the outside.

What can you do to add some flavor? Honestly, I don't think you can add much if you're going to use the slow cooker. Sure, you can inject the shoulder with some sort of marinade (see the section in smoking that follows and the suggested injection combinations at the end of these notes), but I haven't seen the benefits from that treatment like I do when I smoke a Boston butt. Though I'm missing a microscopic analysis and molecular white paper on the subject, I think it's because all the marinade just renders out with the fat, so, again, in the end you've still really only bathed the outside of your butt in far more fat than flavor. Sure, you can also drain off the fat from time to time, but if you use a slow cooker as it's intended in a set-it-and-forget-it mode—I put my Boston butt in the device in the morning before I leave for work and when I come home, *voila*, dinner is served—this isn't really practical. Brining for 24 hours the night before can add some flavor, but, as with the injection, I find going that extra mile is best left for smoking as most of the brining benefit gets lost in the rendered fat.

If you don't mind a little extra work, then removing the roast from the slow cooker and its wading pool of hot fat a couple hours *before* the shoulder is done, injecting it then, double-wrapping in foil, and finishing in a low-temp oven (250- to 275-degree-ish) for a couple hours can help. However, I find a quicker way to get where I'm going is to let the slow cooker do its job, cooking until I have the fall-off-the-bone pulled pork consistency. I then remove the meat from the cooker, leaving all the fat behind, and crisp up the hunks of pork in a fry pan as I need it, along with a generous amount of sea salt and cracked black pepper and maybe some minced garlic or the whites and greens of sliced green onions. Once I've got those pieces of still oh-so-tender pork sizzling and crispy brown on the outside, I can then add any additional seasoning or sauces whatever recipe I'm creating requires. Ta-da, the slow cooker has done all the hard work, while my minimal time over the stove produces all the flavor I could want.

All this said and done, there are a few ways to use the slow cooker to create pulled pork that has enough flavor so you don't need to do anything with it after it's cooked—except eat it. One of these is to use a deeply flavored soda such a Coca-Cola or Dr. Pepper; I used an organic black cherry soda in some ribs I did in the slow cooker (recipe for "Country Ribs With Black Cherry Red Wine Reduction and Gorgonzola" on page 57) with great results. Lots of Southern recipes I come across for pork use Coke or Dr. Pepper, which imparts a really nice sweetness and also tenderizes tougher cuts than a shoulder (no surprise there, coming from products that eat battery acid). The other method I like is to go the 30-cloves of garlic approach. This is an idea I actually took from a slow cooker brisket recipe which, quite literally, used that much garlic. It's enough to flavor most of the meat quite well, even with the vast quantity of rendered fat it ends up being bathed in, because that fat will be so utterly infused with the mellow, nutty, and buttery flavors of the garlic as it, too, slow cooks. Add in plenty of salt and cracked black pepper, and good measure of garlic powder (which has a different profile than fresh garlic), and you should end up with a well-flavored pile of pulled pork. The key to either method is to make several very deep cuts in the shoulder roast—and I do mean deep, down to the bone. You're going to end up shredding, chopping, or thin slicing (depending on how done you prefer yours) the roast in the end, so there's no sense retaining the roast as a whole for some grand presentation as you would with a crown roast. What you gain from these cuts is exposure to much more of the meat since you've increased the surface area exposed to your flavor enhancers such as soda or garlic.

To be honest, the slow cooker is my go-to Boston butt tool during much of the winter. While I like the flavor of pork roasted in the oven better, I have a gas oven that runs off a large, expensive-to-fill propane tank outside the house, so I resist running that oven for long periods of time to keep the refills on the tank down to a minimum. I do have two large smokers, both of which are electric, but the house I'm leasing as I finish the second half of this book is devoid of outside electrical outlets, which means I have to run a long, outside extension cord through an open window or door to operate either unit. Obviously, this is practical in the spring, summer, and early fall of New England, but not so much when the cool days of autumn give way to the freezing winter days. The slow cooker is also good if you don't have a smoker and don't want to heat up your house with an oven that's on for several hours, say, during the middle of August. Truly, this appliance has a place when it comes to preparing pulled pork (as well as many other cuts)—just be aware of its limitations.

If you do not have a smoker of any size or shape, this is the way to turn a fresh off the pig pork shoulder into barbecue-ready pulled pork.

As with anything in the kitchen, there are numerous ways to get the job done. You can start with a sear in a very hot oven—450 degrees—and get the outside sizzling and cracking and browning up nicely before you drop the temperature down low—300 on down to 250 degrees—and let it cook through over several hours. You can also do this in reverse, starting with a low oven and then finishing it off with a high sear. With either, you may need to tent the roast with foil at some point to prevent over-browning (especially if you want to go the route that ends with a sear and produces the perfect crust).

While both these methods produce great results, I don't like using either of them if I don't have to. Why? Because they make a mess in the oven thanks to the spatter of fat during the high heat stage. All that spattering, super-heated fat also produces nasty, smelly smoke that gets in your clothes, your hair, the kitchen curtains, the throw rug under the kitchen table, and the dogs' fur (not that they seem to mind). The method I prefer instead is to use a slow, steady, constant low-temperature roast.

To begin, I set the shoulder, fat cap side up, in a roasting rack like you'd use for a chicken. I set that rack in my favorite deep-sided lasagna pan. This eliminates the rendered fat bath problem you get with the slow cooker method. Eliminating the fat bath also means you can rub or inject the roast with just about anything of your preference and taste the results of those efforts. Either way, what you want to achieve by oven-roasting—and which you most certainly cannot achieve in the slow cooker—is a great crust on the outside. This is *completely* attainable without the high heat sear. No, it won't be bark like you'll get from smoking—it won't be with the high heat sear, either, so no loss there—but it will be some of the tastiest pork you'll have ever put in your mouth. (By the way, one of the best rubs I've done for oven-roasted pork like this is a liberal one of McCormick's Montreal steak seasoning, which is heavy on the big crystal salt and cracked black pepper. Easy-peasy and produces terrific results.)

How long in the oven? Well, depends on several things, not the least of which is how pull-apart you prefer your pork. Most of the time, I want mine to fall off the bone the minute I try to take the roast out of the pan. Other times I'll want to be able to slice it thin, the deepest part of the roast still slightly adhering to the bone, though not so much that I need decisive, concentrated work with a carving knife to separate the two. Set your oven somewhere between 250 and 300 degrees. My last roast was a nine-pounder and, at four-and-half hours at 300, the meat was very tender but a little bit still stuck to the bone—I could pull it off the bone with my fingers, no knife needed, but it didn't fall off the bone in its own. Obviously, if you go lower than 300 or have a larger shoulder, it's going to take longer. (You can always tent the roast in the pan with aluminum foil at some point if you want to stop a perfectly browned but not quite cooked roast from getting too brown and dried out.) The outside crust formed with that thick rub of Montreal steak seasoning was, in a word, *divine*. I spent ten minutes once the roast had rested a while out of the oven, simply pulling off hunks of hot, savory pork and wiping the grease away from my mouth. Addictive stuff right there.

SMOKING

Is there anything as heavenly as smoked meat? I don't care whether it's beef, chicken, or pork; smoking meat is like adding an irresistible perfume to an already beautiful woman. Intoxicating.

Not to beat a dead pig here, but, again, there are about a million ways to smoke a Boston butt (or any other cut of pork, for that matter). I smoke one just about every other weekend outside of the winter months, and while I do prepare the meat with a variety of ingredients, what it all comes down to is dry rub versus wet rub versus injection. Here's how I get each done, though feel free to mix it up. There's no law out there that says you can't inject and do a dry or wet rub as well. Heck, sometimes I use all three when I feel like getting my hands dirty. Also, remember that you can dry rub, wet rub, and inject any pork shoulder you're roasting in the oven on a rack that keeps the roast from bathing in its own fat; you can also inject a shoulder for the slow cooker, but, as I've explained, wet and dry rubs will mostly be a waste in this kitchen top appliance.

DRY RUBS

When I choose to go with a dry rub and create an exceptional bark on my pork shoulder, I will generally brine the pork for 24 to 48 hours first. To brine, you'll need a vessel capable of allowing your shoulder to become completely submerged. Most of the Boston butt shoulders I cook are in the nine-pound range; a whole shoulder—Boston butt and picnic cut un-separated—can go as large as 17 pounds or more. I have a 48-quart Igloo square Ice Cube cooler that works grandly for this and eliminates me having to empty half my refrigerator to make room for a brining shoulder.

No surprise, brines can be made in dozens of varieties. Depending on what I'm doing with the pork, mine will be herbed-based (Williams-Sonoma makes an awesome rosemary brine mix), apple cider vinegar-based (for traditional pulled pork where I come from in Virginia), beer-based, and I've even seen a recipe from Alton Brown that called for molasses. What they all have in common are salt and sugar. Beyond that, pick the flavors you like best.

To brine, prepare your liquid, put it and your Boston butt in the vessel so that the meat is submerged, and either add enough ice to keep it cold (my cooler method) or stick it in your fridge for 24 to 48 hours. The only thing I'll tell you to keep in mind is that brining does add flavor, in addition to its tenderizing effects, so keep the brining elements in proportion to your water and ice. In other words, don't add so much water or ice that you dilute the brine to an ineffective state.

One more note: If you do not have a vessel big enough to allow your meat to be completely covered, make sure you turn the meat every four to five hours so that its entire surface area gets the necessary treatment at some time or another. I would also go with a longer brine, if this is the case.

For the rubs themselves, while I've listed a bunch of combinations at the end of this section, the combinations themselves have no set components. If you like your smoked pig reach-for-a-cold-beer spicy, add more cayenne, paprika, and hot sauce. Tarter? Go heavier on the dried mustard or citrus peels. Like sweet Memphis-style better? Then go heavier on the brown sugar component. Finally, for a lip-smacking roast shoulder that works in making the finished product agreeable to a variety of other recipe creations, keep your rub simply to good coarse salt, cracked black pepper, and ground garlic and onion powder.

WET RUBS

These are really so much fun and there are really only a couple of loose rules when working with them.

First, keep your wet rubs thick. Not only do you not want such a rub to run right off the roast before you pop it in the smoker (or oven), but you also don't want the heat to immediately render the viscosity of your rub to that of water and cause it to run off to the bottom of the drip pan before it has a chance to impart its flavor to the meat. Of course, a thinner version can be used as a marinade for 24 to 48 hours (sometimes longer) before you cook, so no harm no foul if you don't mix up a batch quite the way you want it; you'll just have to delay your cooking time a bit or baste with a too-loose wet rub every hour or so like you would a turkey. That, of course, will extend your smoking time, since every time you open your smoker's door or raise its lid, you lower the temperature and it'll need time to rise back up.

Beyond the consistency of the rub, there are two other things to be cautious of in your wet rub creations. For rubs that are lemon, lime, or orange citrus-based, carefully balance those tarter tones with sugar and heat, as too much of these puckery flavors can leave you with a bitter and even dry experience on the taste buds. Second, go easy on the Worcestershire and soy sauces in those wet rubs that star these ingredients. They have a high salt content, and adding too much additional sea or table salt will absolutely ruin the finished shoulder and you will curse yourself for having to throw away nine pounds of inedible meat.

INJECTIONS

You will, of course, need a special meat injector for this. Amazon sells them, as do most dedicated cooking tool stores and retailers like Cabela's and Bass Pro shops. Most come with two needles, one with multiple small holes along its shaft for use with thin liquid-only injections, and the other with a solid shaft and a single, elongated outlet at the tip that allows the passage of thicker injection formulas and those with pieces of red pepper flakes and the like that would otherwise clog up smaller holes.

I have to give you fair warning. Unless you're highly skilled at injecting, this is usually a pretty messy process. Getting the marinade into the injector is rarely a trouble-free process; none I've used work with the efficiency of a true hypodermic that draws up liquid into the holding receptacle in one smooth pull of the plunger. It is especially difficult with injections that use hot ingredients, like melted butter and honey, as they cause the same pressure build-up problem in the injector body as

hot ingredients in a capped blender do. I strongly suggest that you have a deep sink, paper towels, and an apron in hand, as well as clothes you don't care about staining. A good supply of counter cleaner is also recommended; I've had to scrub injection off the ceiling and cabinets more than once. Ugh.

Once you've gotten an injector full of sauce, how you inject the meat is important. You really want to poke as few holes as possible into the *surface* of the meat. So how do you get the marinade into as much of the inside of the roast as you can? By pushing the needle into the meat at different angles within a single point of entry. Make your first plunge, inject the liquid until you feel resistance or it starts to ooze back out a bit. Pull the needle part way out and then push it back in, but in a different angle. You should be able to get three, four, or maybe even five shots of marinade into your meat per single insertion hole.

When you are injecting, if you feel more than the gentle resistance you'd expect from pushing liquid into the density of raw meat, stop depressing the plunger and pull out. Force it and I promise you'll be wearing more marinade than you ever thought possible, for the marinade you're pushing in will travel right back out your insertion hole and across your face and chest at a higher speed and pressure than that at which it first entered. It will not be pretty, and cayenne in your eye will make you want to die.

I usually inject my roasts when they're sitting on a large cutting board with a drain trough around the edge. Marinade will ooze out, and you'll be thankful for the drain trough when it does. Know that when your injection has honey or butter in it, it's going to cool quickly and become very sticky. (If I'm injecting a roast for the oven, I set the roast in the rack over the pan first, so that the pan catches any of the drips.) Whether sticky or viscous, rub the marinade that oozes out and any leftover marinade you didn't inject all over the body of your shoulder. When it comes to cooking an injected shoulder, as you might imagine, there's no neat and tidy way to get the roast into your smoker without leaving a smear of marinade on everything you touch, so have a roll of paper towels prepared. Go ahead, ask me how I know about this.

Now, onto the actual smoking itself. I know I said that I have two, but I actually have three smokers. One of them is a dome-topped, coated aluminum arrangement from the bake ware company Nordic Ware. Intended for use with any stovetop burner, it works *remarkably* well, proving that not everything has to be complicated to be good. They cost around $80, give or take, from a dozen or more online retailers. Its only drawback is its size. You must be able to fit the lid tightly so that the smoke stays inside the unit, so a large Boston butt isn't generally going to work in this smoker. It does do a fabulous and relatively quick job on loin roasts, boneless pork picnic roasts, chickens, fish, and partial beef brisket portions. I highly recommend adding this to your list of kitchen gadgets if you like smoking but don't want to or can't add an independent upright unit to your backyard patio or porch. Not only does it work as well as it does, it gives you a chance to add a little smoky goodness to weeknight dinners because the cuts that will fit in the smoker don't take hours to cook.

For the longer smokes, including my bone-in Boston butts, I use one of two electric units. I have a large, digitally controlled unit from Bradley and a slightly smaller unit from the brand Cajun Injector (a brand you may recognize from its pre-loaded, disposable meat injectors and marinade lines). Both do a great job.

I do not have a wood-burning smoker. I want one, but most of them tend to be quite large and I don't cater professionally, compete, or cook for large crowds, so it hasn't been necessary for me to invest in one. I also don't own a propane-fueled smoker; that option became less attractive after I learned from everyone I talked to that somehow, some way, there will always be a hint of the propane in the smoke taste. Maybe that's true, maybe it's not, but all I know is that I don't want to invest in one to find out.

After two summers of steadily working on my version of smoked Boston butt perfection, here's the procedure I favor most. When I'm jonesin' for a pulled pork sandwich, I inject a marinade of butter, apple cider vinegar, cayenne, and a couple other things. I'll do maybe a simple rub of garlic powder, onion powder, cayenne, chili powder, and salt on the outside, then slide the butt into the smoker set for somewhere between 215 and 250 degrees. Remember, this is smoking, and low and slow is the rule. Sure, both smokers allow for much higher temperatures, but with high heat you'll be roasting your meat rather than gradually allowing smoke to flavor it. Also, I don't bother with filling the drip pan with water or other liquid and aromatics. It's one more thing to get sloppy with and I don't think it provides a benefit with this cut of meat. Maybe leaner meats and vegetables, but not one so generously fatted as a Boston butt (or beef brisket). To each their own—you certainly can't hurt anything by having a pan of liquid in your smoker to impart a little steam.

For the average nine-pound Boston butt, I'll go six hours in the smoker, with a dose of smoke every hour for the first three hours. The wood I use depends on the flavor profile I'm working in. I use oak and mesquite for roasts done up Tex-Mex spicy; apple and cherry woods for roasts treated with citrus, fruits, and herbs; and hickory for something in between that sassy and sweet range.

Know that you can overdo the smoke and end up with a roast that's cooked properly but has a slightly to very unpleasant bitterness to the bark and first inch or so of meat beneath it. If you haven't spent a lot of time working with a smoker, you're going to need to experiment with the wood type, the number of times you expose the meat to fresh smoke, and the duration of those exposures. (Note: A smoker like the digital unit I have from Bradley utilizes palm-sized compressed discs of wood that are fed automatically into the smoker every 20 minutes for however long I tell it to do so. The Cajun Injector smoker uses either wood pellets made for a smoker—*not* the waxed pellets you use in your pellet stove to heat your rec room—or wood shavings that sit in a tray over a heating element in the bottom of the smoker body and slowly burn without igniting into flames. I control the smoke in the Cajun Injector smoker by adjusting the amount of wood shavings I use and how often I replenish them.)

After the first six hours in the smoker, I bring a large carving board outside to my work area and spread a large swath of heavy-duty aluminum foil over it. Do *not* skimp on this. It needs to be the good stuff, Reynold's, not a cheap grocery store brand, and it needs to be the heavy-duty kind—trust me on this. I remove the roast from the smoker, place it on the middle of the foil, and bring the foil up around it like the folds of a loosened paper cupcake wrapper. I then pour over the roast any leftover or extra marinade I've made and finish enclosing the roast in the foil. Next I wrap the whole thing in a second layer of heavy-duty foil. I can't tell you why, but two layers make a better butt. I have never had a butt or picnic dry out with two layers of foil, as I had once with one layer, so two is what I go with now, without exception.

Back in the smoker the double foil-wrapped butt goes. No more smoke is needed now, of course, since it wouldn't penetrate the foil. What's important now is to let the butt continue its gradual cook at that low temperature. This sometimes achingly slow process—well, achingly when you're hungry, 'cause it all smells damn good at this point—works to break down all that heavy connective tissue within the shoulder to become the succulent, finger-licking, wet-nap-needing hunk of porky heaven you know it's going to be. I will go anywhere from another six to eight hours (12 to 15 hours total, depending on the size of the shoulder), then remove it to sit on a cutting board in the kitchen for at least an hour before peeking inside and pulling off a hunk. You can let it sit longer—between the two layers of foil and the size of the shoulder, that baby can hold its heat for a long while. Heck I've set one on the counter late at night after getting a late start smoking in the morning and still have the center of the roast warm the next morning, And pull-apart easy? Oh, you betcha. In fact, "effortless" would be how I'd describe the shredding of a pork shoulder smoked thusly.

As you'll see from the recipes in the shoulder section of this book, what you can do with leftover pulled pork after you've tired of pulled pork sandwiches is limited only by your imagination. Also, as this long discussion has revealed, you don't need a smoker, but I highly recommend one (out of the two electrics, the Cajun Injector model ran me right around $200 from Amazon and it has performed flawlessly with regular use for more than two years now, and that includes on my deck in Wisconsin in some very, *very* cold weather). No matter how you go about it, this biggest cut of pork is sure to be your new best friend in the kitchen. It offers variety in cooking, variety in flavor, and variety in uses. How much more could you ask from the forearm of a pig?

DRY RUB COMBINATIONS

1. Brown sugar, cayenne, cumin, garlic powder, onion powder, paprika, salt, cracked black pepper, chili powder
2. Cumin, coriander, cinnamon, nutmeg, espresso powder, with or without cayenne and brown sugar
3. Lemon peel, light brown sugar, crushed fennel seed, salt, white pepper. Orange peel can be substituted for the lemon peel, or you can use both along with lime peel
4. Dry ground mustard, garlic powder, onion powder, cayenne, salt, crushed red pepper flakes, cracked black pepper, lemon peel
5. Dried Mexican oregano, cumin, crushed coriander seed, garlic powder, chili powder. Brown sugar optional—let the heady, sweet taste of Mexican oregano really shine in this one. Be generous with this herb and minimize the other ingredients

WET RUB COMBINATIONS

1. Apple cider vinegar, crushed red chili flakes, minced onion, catsup. Alternately you can use molasses in place of the catsup, but either way I go easy on the sweet, heavy on the vinegar and chili flakes.
2. Apple cider vinegar, yellow mustard, crushed red chili flakes, onion powder, garlic powder, crushed garlic, minced onions, salt. Brown sugar optional.
3. Orange juice, brown sugar, red chili flakes, cumin, garlic powder, salt
4. Lime juice, cumin, garlic powder, chili powder, paprika, brown sugar, Worcestershire sauce, salt, cracked black pepper
5. Any bottle of oil-based salad dressing—but not with cheese—such as Italian, raspberry vinaigrette, balsamic vinaigrette, etc. Complimentary herbs such as thyme, rosemary, oregano, and others can also be added, and you should certainly add a good amount of sea salt and cracked black pepper to the mix.

INJECTIONS

1. Butter, cayenne, honey, onion powder, garlic powder
2. Soy sauce, honey, ground ginger, garlic powder, onion powder
3. Butter, sea salt, black pepper
4. Apple cider, apple cider vinegar, catsup, onion powder, garlic powder, cayenne
5. Dark beer (like Guinness), leftover morning coffee, cinnamon, clove, dark brown sugar or molasses, dried ground chipotle pepper or smoked ancho chili pepper, salt, ground black pepper
6. Orange juice, apple cider vinegar, lemon juice, lime juice, garlic powder, salt, light brown sugar or white table sugar
7. Pineapple juice, lime juice, Worcestershire sauce, cayenne, salt
8. Coca-Cola, Dr. Pepper, black cherry cola either by themselves but better with butter, cayenne, and salt.
9. Butter, apple cider vinegar, and your favorite hot sauce (I'm partial to Crystal, Cholula, and the green Tabasco).
10. All sorts of salad dressings and bottled barbecue sauces. Take your pick, just stay away from the chunky salad dressings that won't be pushed through your injector needle, and likely the ones with cheese in them, such as bleu cheese and Caesar. Okay, maybe the Caesar . . . off to the grocery store to find out!

BACON—LEAVE THE FRYING PAN BEHIND

What follows is reworked from part of a dissertation I wrote for my first book, *The Big Book of Bacon*. I can do this for a couple reasons. One, it doesn't count as plagiarism if you're copying your own words (especially if you admit to it up front). Second, there's no need to reinvent the wheel. I started working on this book hot on the heels of completing that first one, and the world of bacon has hardly been revolutionized in the hot-minute interim between the two. What I wrote then is how it still works now, and since bacon is an integral part of several recipes here—including the precious fat rendered from high-quality bacon—it's worth going over what I discovered was a better way to cook this succulent piece of pig.

BAKING BACON

Some time ago, I bemoaned to my bacony friends on Facebook that, while I loved all things bacon, I had issues with the aftermath. Well, more than issues. When you get right down to it, I *loathe* the grease spatter. I hated it on the glass stovetop I had when I wrote the bacon book, and I double-triple-dog hate it on the convoluted gas stove top I use now here in Connecticut. Then there's the ugly, congealed nastiness in the pan, not to mention the kitchen sponge that will never *ever* return to its full usefulness once you've cleaned said pan with it. Love/hate, hate/love. I was torn.

And then someone suggested baking bacon in the oven.

Now, I've been around the butcher block a time or two, and one look at my burgeoning kitchen cabinets will tell you there's nothing I truly need from Williams-Sonoma anymore, but I had never heard of baking bacon. I doubted my friends' advice.

"Gawd, it's bad enough cleaning the stovetop, the oven's got to be worse," I commented on a Facebook post.

"There's actually no spatter at all this way!" came the reply.

"Okay, but I don't want to miss the aroma of it cooking," I whined.

"You won't! You can still smell it, there's just no mess!"

And, so, I tried it. What follows is how the first two trials went and, I have to admit, this is the way to go.

After Googling a bunch of oven-baked bacon processes—foil or parchment paper, 375 degrees or 425, each slice of bacon touching each other or allow space between—here's how it came down after a couple weeks of experimentation using several pounds of bacon of varying thickness.

I use a preheated 380-degree oven. Now, unless I'm baking bread, cakes, or pies, I rarely preheat, but, with bacon, it yields more consistent results and helps get the timing down, especially when you're cooking more than one pound to, say, feed a crowd.

In my arrangement, I lay the strips of a full pound of bacon, edges of the strips touching each other, on a large, foil-covered jellyroll pan. I like my bacon cooked but not crispy across the board, a little wiggly still is what I go for. To get that for normal, kind of thin bacon, I'll let the tray cook, on average, about 17 minutes. Medium-thick will run closer to 25 minutes, and really thick-cut bacon can run over 30. Anything beyond that 17-minute mark I keep a close eye on, checking the pan every couple minutes until I get to the doneness level I desire.

If you've ever cooked more than a couple strips of bacon in your life, you'll know that the fat content in the average, grocery store-purchased one-pound pack can be 99.9-percent fat with a thin edge of meat showing under the package's cleverly placed internal cardboard flap, it could be really meaty through the majority of the center with really, solid, white fat ends, or anywhere in between.

It's a crap shoot—something pork processors clearly understand, or they'd design their packages to actually reveal what's inside. Anyway, cook enough bacon and sooner or later you're going to end up with a really fatty pound. Not a problem, it'll still taste good, but you will want to take your tray of bacon somewhere at the 15-minute mark and pour off the excess fat. If you don't do this, you just end up boiling the bacon to death in its own fat, and it will be damn near impossible to get it to crisp to any degree.

One other caveat: with really thick bacon, you will probably want to take tongs and turn the strips over when they've reached the halfway point in their cooking. Why? Because the side against the foil will brown and crisp up nicely but the topside will remain decidedly undercooked if you don't. This is not something I experience with thinner bacon slices.

BACON BRANDS

This might be a good time to talk about bacon brands. I've experimented with probably 20 brands by now. Among these I sampled Patrick Cudahy (which had a distinct, artificial—almost chemical—smoke taste to it that I did not care for); Wright Brand (my absolute top pick, but, sadly, mostly an East Coast brand and not available much where I live); the offerings from several different private butchers (if you have a private butcher convenient enough to you, by all means, give their bacons a try—they tend to be better priced per pound than the store brands, they tend to be thicker cut, and they tend to be more deeply smoke-flavored, if that appeals to you); Gwaltney and Smithfield (again, mostly available on the East Coast by my experience and certainly worth buying if they're available to you); some off brand one of my grocers in Wisconsin carried called CornKing (good flavor, but wildly inconsistent meat-to-fat ratios, so, if you get a really fatty package, the shrinkage is stupendous); Plumrose, a brand I've found in Connecticut; Oscar Meyer (just fine, not a thing wrong with it); and my grocers' own store-brand (better than the CornKing, but the same criticism still applies, and I'd anticipate your store-brand would be the same—you'll have to debate the price savings against the quality, but my biggest criticism of these low-rent types is that they're just inconsistent).

I tend to use Farmland most, as I find it to be the most consistent bacon in the $5 to $6 a pound range, with Oscar Meyer running a close second. If one's not on sale, I buy the other. My one criticism of Oscar Meyer is that one end of the slices in a package almost always seems to be all fat. Sometimes it's heavy enough I simply cut off the solid fat end, so that my bacon's not just swimming in rendered fat as it cooks.

I occasionally take a pound of my butchers' bacons, but they are heavily smoked. While I like that for eating the bacon all by itself, that smokiness tends to become the pervasive flavor profile when worked into a dish, and that's not generally what I'm looking for. The biggest benefit to a private butcher's bacon cut is usually found in the thickness of the slices and the meatiness of the bacon. Sometimes it's nearly ham-like, something I don't find at all unpleasant.

That brings me back to the low-rent off-brands. In general, unless you just gotta have bacon and really need to save that extra dollar a pound, I'd skip them. Not only do the slices tend to be super thin—sometimes you can see light through them!—they also shrink so much that that, if you need a couple cups of cooked bacon for one of these recipes in this book or your own concoctions, you're going to end up cooking three packs instead of two of one of the better brands, and then your savings have just plum gone out the window.

On the other end of the spectrum are those so-called "gourmet" bacons. Okay, so they're flavored with this or smoked with that. That justifies $10, $12, $15 or more a pound? Oh, and that pound you see may not actually be a pound. I've seen some purveyors selling 12- or 13-ounce packages—that weight listed only in the small print—at exorbitant prices, well past that $10 mark. Save yourself the trouble. Either make your own (there are plenty of charcuterie books out there to tell you how to do this, but really it's not much more difficult than taking a slab of pork, curing it in curing salts for a week, then smoking it for a few hours), or simply spice or sweeten up your bacon before baking.

The lesson here, really, is that, if this book inspires you to work bacon into more of your dishes, then experiment a little. The worst you'll end up doing is cooking a second batch, and what's so bad about that?

ADDITIONAL BACON COOKING TIPS

Here are a few things about cooking bacon I've discovered over the years.

1. Try to cook a full pound of bacon at one time, laying the slices on the foil so that they're touching. If you must cook just a few slices, reduce your cooking time and keep an eye on the oven. Just a few slices spaced apart cook much faster than a full pan.

2. I finally settled on a 380-degree preheated oven. When I set mine at 375 degrees, the bacon, no matter what type, seemed to boil along in its own rendered fat, never really quite getting the edges crisp or browning. Even when I poured off the grease, the bacon took too long to get done at 375 degrees, up to 35 minutes for regular slices. That might not be an issue for you if you're not feeding a crowd and need to make several batches, but it might be important if you're timing your bacon to be done at the same time other dishes you're cooking are finished.

    Raising the temperature developed another set of problems. Not only did I get a lot of oven spatter, which caused my oven and, eventually, the entire house to be filled with bacon smoke, when I boosted the temp to something like 400 or 425, cooking time becomes *very* unpredictable. If you're not keeping an eagle eye on your pan, you can go from almost there to burnt in a flash. All this said, every oven is different. You need to play with yours to find out what works best for you. However, regardless what temperature and duration you settle on, preheating is a must. You will *never* get predictable results if you start with a cold oven.

3. When cooking for a large crowd and working up several pounds of bacon, there's no need to switch the foil out in between batches. I routinely cooked three to four pounds of bacon every weekend in the course of developing this book and the first, and so long as you pour the fat off in between batches, you're good to go. The foil does get pretty dark towards the end of the third pound, due to all those little bits and pieces continuing to bake, so, if your crowd is army sized and you need to cook much more than that, then, yes, I would swap out the foil to keep new batches from taking on that burnt flavoring. Otherwise, so long as you don't pierce the foil with a fork while you're lifting off finished slices, your cleanup should be effortless—just ball up the foil once the fat has cooled and solidified, throw it in the trash, and put your still-clean jellyroll pan back in the cabinet.

4. If you're making your bacon ahead of time for something like burgers or sandwiches and intend the bacon to be hot when you do use it in the dish, undercook it a little bit. When you're close to serving, spread the mostly cooked bacon across a foiled cookie sheet and reheat for a few minutes at 350 (or lower). It takes almost no time at all for bacon to reheat and it continues to cook as it does, thus my advice to undercook a bit when you're first whipping up a pound. Do *not* reheat in the microwave. Microwaving reheats far too quickly and the spatter on the inside of the appliance will drive you to madness, I don't care how well you think you've covered the bacon while you're nuking it.

5. You might be tempted to go with organic bacon. I've also seen something called "uncured, nitrate-free" bacon, but that's like saying "non-dairy ice cream" or "meatless hamburger." There is no such thing. If it's not cured with that pink, nitrate-containing curing salt, then it's not bacon. Yes, some bacon can be had that's been cured with things like celery salt and such, but I tried a couple of these and was very disappointed. One disaster I remember in particular was a pound of Oscar Mayer's new Smoked Uncured Bacon. It developed *terrible* shrinkage—think a manly man gone all polar bear plunge—and that shrinkage was *not* due to the overcooking. In fact, even at the still-flexible stage I like my bacon, I was left with what could only be described as miniature bacon strips. They weren't good for anything but a couple finger sandwiches with the Queen. I tried a couple other organic and uncured bacons, but the results were the same for all. I was left with mini-me strips no matter what I tried. Not only that, they were all excessively salty and yet managed to lack the deep, bacony taste we cook the darn stuff for to begin with. If that weren't enough to dissuade you, consider this: The organic and uncured bacons I found were all sold in those deceptive 12-ounce packages and at prices approaching $10 or more a pound. Ridiculous.

SPICED AND CANDIED BACONS

Peppered bacon and maple-flavored bacon are routinely found in every grocery store I've ever been in. But making your own flavored bacon is so simple, you'll wonder why you haven't tried it before. All you need is a pound of bacon, a gallon Ziploc bag, and whatever flavoring ingredient you like. For cracked pepper, I'd go with about two tablespoons of medium-fine grind. For hot-sauced flavor, a quarter-cup or up to a half ought to do it. For candied bacon, you'll need about a half-cup of light brown sugar. Whichever route you're going, separate your strips of bacon and put them one at a time into the Ziploc bag. Add in your flavoring, zip the bag shut, and shake and massage until the strips are evenly coated. From there, simply bake as usual on your foil-wrapped jellyroll pan.

A couple notes on candied bacon. First, keep a really close eye on the bacon, but don't let the color fool you. Because the brown sugar caramelizes and combines with the rendered fat, it gets dark before it's done. You may want to lower the oven temp just a tad, and you'll certainly want to pour off excessive renderings so it doesn't start to burn. Second, this stuff is ridiculously sticky when it's done. Better to place it on wax paper to cool than your standard paper towel. Finally, when it does cool, the bacon will be very stiff, thanks to the cooled, caramelized sugar coating. Thick bacon can resemble jerky in texture—but it won't matter, because this stuff is beyond addictive.

BACON GREASE—IT'S A GOOD THING

When cooking multiple batches of bacon, you'll need to pour off the rendered, liquid fat in between. Find a heat-proof glass container, cup the foil at one edge of your jellyroll pan to form a kind of spout, and merely tip the pan up to pour. (Do I have to tell you to do this with potholders on your hand? Well, there you go.)

I use a spare two-cup Pyrex measuring cup or one of my many ceramic mixing bowls and save my grease unless my pour-off has a lot of blackened pieces in it. You can stick in the fridge if you like, but, in a cool kitchen, it really doesn't go bad. If you think you've had yours too long, merely discard the solidified fat in the garbage pail (not down your kitchen drain), and start fresh with the next batch of bacon you make. I use bacon fat all the time for things like sautéing veggies and chicken, just for that little extra boost of flavor. I'll also baste biscuits or bread in it now and again, as well as add some to refried beans made from scratch instead of lard), and I'll stir a dab into my rice cooking in a rice cooker. I dunno, it just adds something you can't get with anything else.

BACON ENDS—OR AS I CALL IT, BACHAMEND

What are bacon ends? They are everything from the cured and smoked pork belly that doesn't make it into nice, neat rows of display case-perfect slices or that fit conveniently and uniformly into pre-sized vacuum-packed bags. They are, indeed leftovers.

You are likely going to have to find a butcher for bacon ends, as its uncoordinated state just doesn't meet the definition of most grocery store fare. There are some packaged brands, but the problem with these is that they tend to be uncured. My butcher in Wisconsin smoked his own bacon and packaged the leftover trimmings (the mark of a good butcher, in my opinion, is one who doesn't let things go to waste). They came vacuum packed in quantities roughly 3 ¼ pounds, and the price per pack ran under $4 a pound—*significantly* less than "pretty" bacon. Based on that alone, bacon ends are worth seeking out, but I've discovered there are some other benefits to it, as well.

When I cut open my first pack, I thought I was going to find lots of bits and pieces. I did not. I found big, meaty, fatty chunks, thick-cut strips that were clearly from the last of a pork belly end run through the slicer, and then these decadently thick, almost steak-like hunks with a thick ridge of ham-like meat that tapered to beautiful white fat at the ends. Together, I came to think of these tidbits as Bachamend.

At home with my first pack, I pondered the un-uniformed pile before me and whipped out one of my bigger Wusthoff knives, chunking up the pile into more or less like-size pieces. I figured that was probably the best way to get it cooked evenly, especially given the array of content that ranged from nearly all meat to nearly all fat.

Spread out on my foil-lined jellyroll tray, I set it in a 385-degree oven for 25 minutes. I checked the tray at 20 minutes, poured off the fat—there's quite a bit, though it's deliciously clear and worth saving—and then set it back in the oven to run out the last five minutes on the timer. Some batches have taken a little longer, but this is the time and temp I get most of it done.

It was love at first bite. Here I had bacon, ham, and pork belly, all in one, with the spectrum of flavor and richness I'd been searching for in the dozens of brands of uniform slices I've bought in the name of this book, but had not quite found. Textures ranged from chewier on the ham side, fatty delight on the pieces that were half-and-half meat and fat, and the insane decadence of perfectly roasted pork belly. Left cold and buttered (yes, *buttered!*) in their own softened fat, they were the ultimate definition of "meat candy" everyone jokes about bacon being; with a cooked tray sitting on the counter and cooling, I could *not* keep my hands off it. Best of all, when cooked and then further chopped up to make easier to incorporate, the bacon ends imparted a depth to other dishes that I don't believe regular strips of bacon are capable of. Top that with the fact that the price per pound is so much less than bacon, it makes a lot of sense to use bacon ends in place of bacon where an appreciable quantity is called for.

Don't get me wrong. Bacon strips will always have a place in my cooking. Truly, I couldn't live without strips, especially when I *do* want a very uniform product that crumbles or purées to great consistency. But sometimes it's hit or miss when it comes to the actual amount of bacon *flavor* they impart, especially when you're trying to balance the texture of a dish against what can be chewy and crunchy bacon bits; the more you reduce bacon in its size, the more the tendency for the flavor it exports to the dish to dissipate. And let's be real, while I don't think most people put enough bacon in a dish that calls for it as an ingredient—seriously, two or three strips on a BLT, what the heck's up with *that?*—when you put too much in, you end up with a greasy, soggy mess that slicks on the tongue and lets no other flavor through.

Bacon ends seem to solve a great deal of that power struggle between texture and flavor. I get the deepness, richness, and distribution of flavor I'm looking for in something like bacon cornbread, but without the hard crunchy bits from crumbled bacon that rather interrupt the bite of such things. Both a compromise and a bonus I hadn't expected in the world of cured pork and pork belly delights, bacon ends are something I'm very glad I discovered. My advice to you? Find a good butcher and experiment with bacon ends should you find them. Well worth your time in the pursuit of bacon love.

RIBS—SORT OF

You will notice a lack of rib recipes in this book. As you might imagine, and if you've read this far, there are a couple reasons for this.

I hate to say this, but I'm not a huge fan of ribs of the baby-back or St. Louis style. Even as a partial rack, they are unwieldy. Sure you can cut them into smaller sections, but I've tried that and I don't think that method works well *before* cooking. Other criticism includes the fact that they offer not a lot of meat for the amount of work put into them, and I don't like the fact that you need to eat them using only your hands. Other than things like hotdogs, brats, Italian sausage grinders, hamburgers, Maryland blue crabs, and fair food that comes on a stick, I am all about the fork and knife. I don't like spice rubs and sauces under my fingernails, around my mouth, and on my face and shirtfront, and I don't like the feeling that I need to take a long hot shower to scrub the grease and stickiness off me afterwards. Thus, if you find me with a plate of ribs in front of me, I'm either extremely intoxicated—or it was the only thing available and I was otherwise going to starve to death.

There's another reason I don't like baby-back and St. Louis ribs much, and that is the connective tissue holding the meat to the rib. It takes a tremendous amount of expertise to cook a perfect rack of ribs that gets the meat tender enough to easily rip off the bone with your teeth and yet doesn't fall off the bone on its own. Such finesse, I believe, is attainable only by those good with this particular cut on the grill or smoker. I am not one of those people. However, if you can't get the baby-back rib jingle from the Applebee's advertisement out of your head, my intent is not to disappoint, but there are as many books on smoking and barbequeing baby-back and St. Louis ribs as there are grills and smokers. You're better off using one of them as your reference guide than any advice I can offer up on these two cuts.

There are a couple recipes for country-style ribs within these pages. For a non-rib lover like me, these recipes turned out to be a delightful surprise. Part tenderloin, part loin and with some really good fat content, this is a rib that takes well to a high-heat sear followed by a braise or a long, comfy sit in a slow cooker. They offer far more meat than the other rib cuts and can make a spectacular presentation.

PORK BELLY

This was a tough one to exclude from the book, but, in the end, I had no choice. I simply couldn't find a reliable source for this specialty cut after I moved to Connecticut, where most of this book was composed.

Pork belly has ridden a trendy wave the past couple years, making an appearance on highly rated televised chef competitions and the menus of gastro pub and five-star restaurants alike. It is decadent stuff, hunks of nearly pure fat that becomes something angels weep for when cooked perfectly. I highly recommend indulging in it every once in a while when you can find it, though I'm pretty sure I couldn't find a cardiologist to go along with that idea. But I can't cook what I can't find and I won't make up something I haven't played with thoroughly, so my apologies for not having this gorgeous bit of pig available for you here. I hope you'll find the rest of the creations here more than make up for its absence.

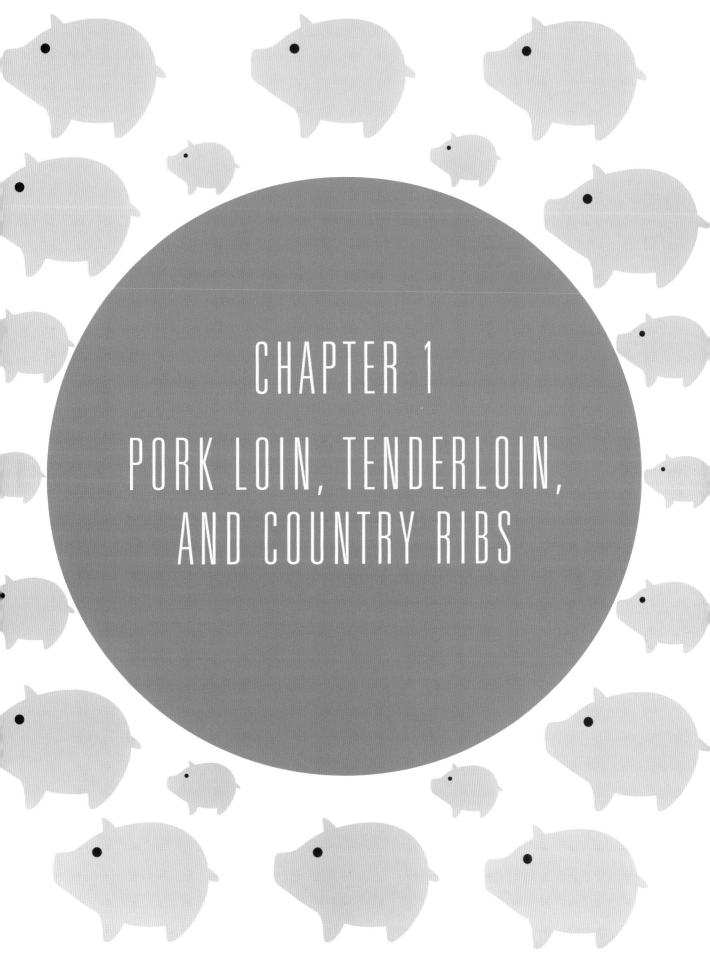

CHAPTER 1
PORK LOIN, TENDERLOIN, AND COUNTRY RIBS

Chili-Rubbed, Salsa-Braised Chops with Spiced Rice, with Two Variations

Pork chops are not one of my favorite pork cuts to cook—they have a decided firmness, a lack of fat, and the fact that damn near everyone overcooks them. I didn't and don't detest them, though, nor do I disdain them like I do ribs (see my comments about ribs on page 34). So, it was time to get with the program and make a few recipes that were good enough so that even *I* might enjoy them.

Here's what you'll need for a dinner for two:

FOR THE CHOPS

2 thick-cut bone-in pork chops
½ cup of flour
1 teaspoon of salt
1 teaspoon of cracked black pepper
1 tablespoon of chili powder
1 tablespoon of bacon fat
1 15-ounce bottle (or close) of your favorite salsa (I used Goya's Hot Salsa Taquera in the 17.6-ounce bottle)

FOR THE CUMIN RICE

2 cups of white, long-grain, fragrant rice (Texmati, Jasmine, etc.)
1 tablespoon of garlic powder
1 tablespoon of onion powder
2 teaspoons of salt
3 tablespoons of ground cumin
1 cup of chopped green onions (whites and greens)
2 cups of chicken broth

INSTRUCTIONS

1. If you need to, thaw your chops.* Mix the flour, salt, black pepper, and chili powder together on a dessert-sized plate, then press the chops down into the seasoned flour, both sides.

2. Preheat your oven to 350. Next, heat either your braiser or a large, oven-proof sauce pan that has a tight-fitting lid over medium-high heat and melt your bacon fat. When the fat is sizzling, swirl your pan to coat the bottom and lay each chop down in the fat. You should hear the prominent hiss of a pan hot enough to sear.

3. Leave your chops on their first side down until they lift away easily with a pair of tongs. If they're sticking to the pan, that side's not ready. In a pan that is hot enough, this should take three minutes or so. When the chop comes away from the pan freely, it should be deeply colored. Repeat with the second side, following the same pull away rule to check for doneness. However, if you started with a frozen chop like I did, know that the *inside* is *not* done yet.

4. As soon as the second side of the chops looks like the first, pour in your salsa over the chops and around, and *immediately* lid the pan and slide the works into the oven for 20 to 30 minutes depending in the thickness of your chops.

5. Meanwhile, cook your rice. I use a rice cooker, but you can do this on a stovetop with a lidded stockpot. Add two cups of liquid to two cups of rice, and throw in your spices and chopped green onions. Cook until done, which should be just about the time your chops finish. They should be piping hot, tender, and juicy.

6. Spoon the cumin-spiced rice into a large dinner bowl, lay a chop on top, and ladle over the cooked down salsa in the braising pan. Add a squeeze of lime wedge over the top or even a dollop of sour cream, then hiss open an ice cold bottle of beer and enjoy.

---

*TIP   Usually, I thaw chops beforehand. However, in my haste I forgot to take them out of the freezer in a timely manner, and I loathe thawing things in the microwave—you always end up cooking some portion of the meat, while the center is still a chunk of meaty ice. Ick. However, I remembered coming across a kitchen hack that said you could throw a frozen piece of meat immediately in a hot pan and end up with a steak perfectly medium-rare on the inside and *not* overdone in the outside. I gave it a whirl. My two chops were out of the freezer an hour before I started to prep them—enough time that they weren't stuck together anymore and a teensy bit moist on the outside. It worked just fine and I'm convinced that I no longer need to fret about remembering to take something out of the freezer in the morning so I can have dinner that night.

HABENERO HAWAIIAN CHOPS

FOR THE CHOPS

2 thick-cut bone-in pork chops
½ cup of flour
1 teaspoon of salt
1 teaspoon of cracked black pepper
1 tablespoon of bacon fat
1 14-ounce bottle of habanero pineapple
marinade*

FOR THE HAWAIIAN RICE

2 cups of white, long-grain, fragrant rice
(Texmati, Jasmine, etc.)
2 cups of chicken broth
1 teaspoon of ground white pepper
1 tablespoon of butter
1 ½ cups of fresh, chunked pineapple
(drained of excess juice)
1 cup of shredded carrot
2 cups of fresh pea shoots
*Optional: 2 cups of shredded habanero or
jalapeño Jack cheese*

---

*TIP   I don't mind buying the occasional bottle of marinade or dipping sauce off my grocer's shelves now and again. If you can find a line of well-made products without a lot of additives and preservatives, it'll cost you less money and time than if you were to make it yourself. Such was the case with a lovely 14-ounce bottle of Terrapin Ridge Farms All Natural Roasted Pineapple Habanero Sauce. Not hard to whip up if you can't find it.

1. Take a 16-ounce can of pineapple or fresh pineapple and crush in a food processor.

2. Put it in a saucepan along with ½ cup sugar (or more to taste), a cup of finely diced sweet onion, a quarter-cup of apple cider vinegar, one finely diced habanero (handle carefully), and bring to a boil.

3. Reduce to low and reduce, stirring frequently, until you have a thick sauce.

1. Preheat your oven to 350 degrees. Prepare your chops as in the chili-rubbed version. Mix flour, salt, and pepper together on a small plate, dredging both sides of the chops through the mix. Sear each side in the bacon fat as above, until each is golden brown and comes away easily from the pan. As soon as the second side is done, pour in your habanero pineapple marinade, *immediately* lid your pan, and slide the braiser into the oven. Leave for 20 to 30 minutes, depending on the thickness of your chops.

2. Meanwhile, cook your rice either on a stove top or in a rice cooker, adding in the rice, chicken broth, and ground white pepper. In a separate sauté pan, warm to medium high and add a tablespoon of butter. Once the pan is hot and the butter well melted, toss in your pineapple chunks. Brown the pineapple lightly, reducing the heat as necessary to keep the butter itself from browning, then add in your shredded carrots and lid the pan. Give it five minutes under the lid, enough to soften the carrots but still keep a bit of texture, then add your hot rice. Toss to combine in the pan and lid it, reducing the temperature to low for five minutes or so or until your chops are cooked. Remove from the heat and add your pea shoots.

3. For service, spoon a generous helping of the pineapple rice into a large bowl or plate and lay on one of the chops. Ladle some of the reduced habanero pineapple sauce from the braising pan over each and sprinkle on pepper Jack cheese. I particularly liked this with one of the super-citrusy Sauvignon Blanc wines from New Zealand.

SWEET GINGER SESAME AND GREEN CURRY RICE

FOR THE CHOPS

2 thick-cut bone-in pork chops
½ cup of flour
1 teaspoon of salt
1 tablespoon of Chinese five-spice
1 14-ounce jar (or close) of sweet ginger sesame sauce (I used the brand House of Tsang)
1 tablespoon of bacon fat

FOR THE GREEN CURRY RICE

2 cups of white, long-grain, fragrant rice (Texmati, Jasmine, etc.)
1 ½-cups of chicken broth
1 15-ounce jar of green curry (I used an 11.9-ounce bottle of the brand Thai Kitchen)
1 tablespoon of garlic powder
1 tablespoon of onion powder
2 teaspoons of salt
Optional: Fried chow mein noodles, chopped raw green onions (whites and greens), a cup of toasted sesame seeds, or all three

INSTRUCTIONS

1. Preheat your oven to 350 degrees. Prepare your chops as in the chili-rubbed version. Mix your flour, salt, and Chinese five-spice mix together on a small plate, dredging both sides of the chops through the mix. Sear each side as above, until each is golden brown and comes away easily from the pan. As soon as the second side is done, pour in your jar or bottle of sweet ginger sesame sauce, *immediately* lid your pan, and slide the braiser into the oven. Again, leave for 20 to 30 minutes, depending on the thickness of your chops.

2. Meanwhile, cook your rice either over the stovetop or in a rice cooker, adding in the rice, chicken broth, jar of green curry sauce, garlic powder, onion powder, and salt. For serving, spoon a generous helping of the finished curry rice into a large bowl or plate and lay on one of the chops. Ladle some of the reduced sweet ginger sesame sauce from the braising pan over each. Sprinkle on fried chow mein noodles if you like, and maybe raw greens and whites from fresh green onions or a sprinkling of toasted sesame seeds. You can certainly go the sake route for an accompanying beverage, though I prefer a top-quality Japanese beer like Asahi Kuronama, Kirin, or Saporro.

Chipotle Corn Cake Stuffed Pork Tenderloin Roll

Out of all the straight cuts of pork, the one that is the most versatile is the loin, particularly the tenderloin, which can be found just about anywhere that sells groceries. The cut you most often see in the general supermarket case are generally pretty large full loins, and packages sometimes contain both sides. It is also easy to find tenderloins that are smaller in size. These days most of them come pre-seasoned and pre-marinated from the big pork suppliers like Hormel. But, if you've read even a smidge of this book, you know I don't play that game. It was off to the butcher I went.

One of the two butchers I use regularly almost always has a good supply of pork cuts, including tenderloin. I looked at what he had, asked the white-aproned gentleman if he had anything bigger. "I want to be able to pound it out and make a roll out of it," I explained to him. Ten minutes later I had a *beautiful* pork tenderloin, butterflied and pounded out, coming over the countertop to me neatly wrapped flat in pristine white butcher paper.

Next stop was the grocery store. Still chilly outside, I decided that something spicy, earthy, and Mexican-y was the way to go. Here's what you'll need:

FOR THE CHIPOTLE MOLE CORN CAKE

2 cups of all-purpose flour
3 cups yellow corn meal
2 teaspoons of baking powder
1 cup of sugar
1 teaspoon of salt
1 ½ cups of milk (plus extra as needed)
2 eggs
1 cup of honey
1 stick of butter, melted
8 ounces of frozen corn, thawed and drained
1 7-ounce can of chipotle peppers in adobe sauce or roasted sweet bell peppers

FOR THE ROLLED PORK TENDERLOIN

1 1 ½- to 2-pound pork tenderloin, butterflied
1 teaspoon of salt
1 teaspoon of cayenne or black pepper
2 tablespoons of light brown sugar
1 bunch of fresh cilantro
Optional: ½ cup of melted honey, 2 tablespoons of sriracha, 1 cup of chicken stock

BUTTERFLYING A PORK TENDERLOIN

If you need to butterfly the meat yourself, here's what you have to do:

1. Set your tenderloin, which should be cylindrical in shape, and, starting a third of the way down from the top of the roll, make a slice horizontally through the length of the meat, stopping short of going through and slicing off the top—leave about a half-inch of uncut meat on the opposite side of where you began your cut. Now, on the opposite side of the loin, this time starting a third of the way up from the bottom, make a horizontal cut through from this side, again leaving about a half-inch of meat un-knived on the side where you made your first cut.

2. With these two cuts, you should be able to gently unfold the loin into three connected sections. Be careful not to tear the meat so that it separates at the slice marks along the loin's length. You want this to remain intact as a single piece of meat.

3. Place the butterflied loin between two sheets of wax paper and pound to a uniform depth. You will pound less at the butterflied junctures; again, be careful not to pound this area so that this "seam" separates. From here, you should be done, but, if you're really uptight about symmetry, you can trim the ends and square up the meat to make a uniform rectangle.

1. Combine the salt, cayenne, and brown sugar. If heat's not your thing, substitute the cayenne with black pepper (though this dish is intended to be spicy). Rub the spices into both sides of your flattened loin. Refrigerate, flat on a plate, until ready to use.

2. Get started on the corn cake batter. Combine the dry ingredients in a stand mixer, saving the salt for last. One at a time, add the milk, eggs, honey, and melted butter, mixing just to combine after each addition. Add your corn and combine. Lastly, add your can of chipotle peppers in adobe sauce. Once again, if heat ain't your thang, either reduce to half a can, substitute it for roasted sweet bell peppers, or eliminate.

3. Grease two regular loaf pans, a 9x13 pan, or a large deep-dish pie plate. Place on a rimmed cookie sheet in case of overflow. Pour in your corn cake batter, and put into a 350-degree oven for 40 minutes to an hour. Remove when the crust is golden and a toothpick in the center comes out clean. Cool until you can handle it with your fingers.

4. While the corn cake cools, take your flattened loin out of the fridge and bring to room temperature. Mince your cilantro, stems and all, and spread evenly across the meat, end to end and side to side. With either a fork or your fingers, tear into the warm corn cake (it should be very moist, even sticky), and distribute it across the cilantro base.

5. Starting with one of the narrow ends of your meat rectangle, roll it away from you like you would a burrito (but without tucking in the ends) or a sushi roll. Place seam side down on your prep board, and tie in three places (both ends and the center) with trussing twine. Stuff any stuffing that falls out.

6. Set it seam side down on a chicken roasting rack that fits in a shallow 9x13 lasagna pan. (Optional: I felt it was missing something, so I poured honey and sriracha sauce over the roast, covering the topside of the roll and letting the sauce ooze down the sides and onto the pan. I also added a little chicken stock to the pan.) Set it in a pre-heated 400-degree oven for 20 minutes, then lower the temperature to 350 and let it go for 25 minutes.

7. Remove when it is beautifully browned and glazed, and let stand for 10 minutes. When ready to serve, slice your roast with a sharp knife (this roll stays together well, thanks to the dense, moist corn cake, which resists crumbling).

8. To serve, I laid a couple of beautiful rounds over a rice and bean mixture that I'd whipped up while the roll was cooling. All you have to do is combine a couple cups of cooked jasmine rice, a can of drained black beans, a cup of cooked diced bacon, and a half bunch of chopped cilantro in a sauté pan and steam. You can also serve the rolls by themselves with glazed carrots or sweet potatoes, which bring a nice counterpoint to the roll's spicy stuffing.

Colby-Bacon Cornbread Stuffed Pork Loin Roast

I went to the butcher the other day, looking for a good-sized pork tenderloin that I could stuff and roll. Kindly, he offered to butterfly a full loin roast for me. Naturally, I gave him the go ahead.

This crowd-pleaser recipe makes quite a meal. You can easily serve five or six people, or four with a couple getting seconds. Pork loin roasts are sizeable, as opposed to the original tenderloin I wanted and that would have served just two or three. Here's what you'll need:

INGREDIENTS

1 3- to 4-pound pork loin roast, butterflied
   (and pounded for tenderizing/thickness
   as necessary)
1 pound of bacon
2 cups of cornmeal
1 cup of white flour (cake flour preferable)
3 teaspoons of fine sea salt
½ cup of light brown sugar

3 teaspoons of baking powder
1 can of creamed corn
1 ½ to 2 cups of whole milk
3 large or Jumbo eggs
2 cups of shredded Colby cheese
2 teaspoons of cracked black pepper
1 ½ teaspoon of cayenne
1 teaspoon of crushed rosemary

BUTTERFLYING A PORK LOIN ROAST

Have your butcher butterfly your pork loin roast. If he has a mechanical pounder on hand, have him tenderize it, too. He should not charge you for this—ever.

If you cannot get your butcher to cooperate with you, you will have to butterfly the pork loin yourself.

1. Set your roast fat side up on a dry cutting board.

2. The ends of the roast are roughly oval in shape. Imagine two lines evenly drawn across that oval, horizontally arranged (parallel to the cutting board) and evenly dividing that oval into three sections.

3. Working along the length of the roast, and with a very sharp knife, work from one edge of the meat along the bottom line—one-third of the way up from the bottom of the roast—cutting through almost to the other side but stopping short about a half- to three-quarters-inch from the edge.

4. Open the roast a bit at the cut, like a book, and insert your knife at the point where you ended the first cut but slicing now in a direction perpendicular to the first cut. You're making an "L"-shaped cut, this second cut half the depth of the meat on that side.

5. Insert your knife at the bottom of this second cut, but now parallel to the first cut, and slice sideways through this two-thirds section of the roast, along/through its length, stopping short of the outside of the roast about a half- to three-quarters-inch. You are, in essence, making the same cut as the first, but from the *inside* of the roast instead of the outside.

6. You should now be able to open the roast at those two cuts. Aid the opening by continuing to gently draw the knife along the original cuts, but you need to have at least a half- to three-quarters-inch of roast uncut. It should be obvious that cutting through the original two cuts all the way to the other side will leave you with pieces of roast, rather than one flat piece.

7. The idea with butterflying is to get the roast to a flat piece of meat, but you also want that piece to be as evenly thick as possible from end to end and side to side. Yes, you're working with a round(ish) piece of meat, so you will often have two half-circle shapes on either end and a rectangular piece in the middle. That's okay, so long as those three pieces are of relatively even thickness, but you want to avoid having the two original cuts cut too deeply, as they can tear when rolling, cooking, and slicing.

1. Make a single cut lengthways along the roast and through the center (again, do not cut all the way through).

2. Open the roast, carefully slicing along your original cut to get it as far open as possible without ripping the roast in two.

3. On one side of the opening, insert your knife into the meat at the cut but perpendicular to it and cut halfway down to the outside of the roast. At the bottom of the slit, begin to work your knife sideways through that half of the meat. As above, you're opening up a third flap of meat from the *inside* of the roast, rather than the outside. Remember to stop short of running your knife all the way through, opening that newly created flap gradually to prevent tearing.

4. Repeat step #3 on the other side of the roast.

5. To better open the roast, gently draw your knife along each of the three slices. In the end, you should have four "sections" with three "joints" where your slicing ended, and hopefully a very evenly thick and flat piece.

None of this is really hard, but it does take some finesse, a really good knife, and patience.

You should also tenderize your butterflied roast to thin it or to make its sections evenly thick. Take a piece of wax paper, cover the meat with the paper smooth side down (the wax paper keeps raw juices from spattering), and whack away as needed with the toothed end of a metal meat pounder, with the meat set on a firm surface like a wood cutting board. It's a good idea to tenderize because the pork loin roast (not the tenderloin) is basically an unsliced pork chop—a dense piece of meat, very white and lean, and can therefore be very tough. Pounding a really thick roast helps, not to mention the fact that it makes rolling a stuffed roast easier.

INSTRUCTIONS

1. Cook your bacon in a 380-degree oven for 17 to 25 minutes on a foil-covered jellyroll pan (see more instructions on page 27–29). When it's done to your liking*, remove the bacon to drain on a plate lined with paper towels. Pour the rendered fat into a heat-proof vessel for future use.

2. While the bacon is draining, start the cornbread by whisking together cornmeal and flour. I prefer cake flour for its lighter texture, but all-purpose works just fine. Whisk in one

teaspoon of salt, then incorporate your brown sugar and baking powder. Add the can of creamed corn, pour in half the milk, and give it a quick mix. Add one of the eggs, mixing again to distribute. Alternate the eggs and milk until you have a fairly thick batter (you should add all the eggs, so end using only the milk you need), but not one so thick that you can't easily work in the shredded cheese for even distribution. Before you work in the cheese, chop your bacon into a fine dice. Once you've got the cheese and bacon prepped, mix both in to distribute evenly.

3. Grease a 9x13 baking dish with either butter, bacon fat, or an all-natural non-stick spray. Pour in your cornbread batter and smooth the top with a rubber spatula. Slide the pan into a pre-heated 350-degree oven for 40 to 50 minutes. The cornbread is done when it's golden brown on top and a toothpick inserted in the middle comes out clean, so check at the 40-minute mark and then every 10 minutes after until done. If the cornbread is getting too brown on the top, put foil across it while it finishes baking through. When done, remove the pan from the oven and set aside until cooled enough to break apart with your fingers.

4. Lightly season the inside of the flattened roast (fat cap should be on the outside), with some of the salt, black pepper, cayenne (just a pinch), and the crushed rosemary.

5. Break up your cornbread and spread it a good inch deep across the roast, leaving an inch of meat without stuffing at one end and two inches at the other. Press the stuffing down so that it's a bit compacted. You can add some pats of soft butter if you like to add extra moisture to the meat if you have a very long butterflied loin roast that will require longer cooking. As you can see from the picture, my roast is rolled up into one circle around the stuffing, rather than spiraling.

6. Starting with the end of the roast that has just one inch without stuffing, roll toward the other end, keeping the roll tight, but not forcing it together or smashing it. It's okay if some stuffing falls out—you can push it back into the ends as you roll.

7. Finish the roll and place it seam side down on your cutting board. Tie with kitchen twine at least three ties (middle and both ends), with two more as necessary for a particularly wide roast. The point is to make the roll as uniform from end to end as possible, without bulging in between the twine pieces, which will gap as they cook and spill out the stuffing. Rub the remaining salt, pepper, and crushed rosemary thoroughly along the outside of the roast and set in a roasting rack over a roasting pan with a cup of water in it.

8. Preheat your oven to 450 degrees. Slide the pan with the roast above it in and let it go for 15 minutes, then drop the temperature back to 350. You'll likely go about an hour, maybe 10 minutes less or more, and the roast should brown nicely after that initial high temp toast. If you feel it's getting too brown and still isn't cooked yet, tent it with foil and check every 10 minutes until done. To determine doneness, insert a probe thermometer into the

meat (not the stuffing) and it should register about 150. Some say 160, but I think that dries out the pork. I actually prefer about 145, as this roast will continue to cook a little when out of the oven. Remove the roast and sit for 15 to 20 minutes under a foil tent.**

9. This is a gorgeous way to do a pork roast. It looks great on the table and plate, it's satisfying without being too heavy, and it has a comforting quality to it. Serve with a light side salad or some fresh green beans and a light, crisp Sauvignon Blanc or Chardonnay (like those from New Zealand), and you'll have a terrific weekend dinner for a warm spring Saturday evening with friends.

---

*TIP I like my bacon a little on the limp side—a little chewy instead of crisp. While you may prefer yours more done, most recipes that incorporate bacon should do so with bacon still in the slightly less than crispy stage. Why? Because bacon continues to cook every time you reheat it, and you don't want to end up with overdone bacon or hard bits.

**TIP We rest meat because it's the right thing to do. It lets the juices, which have pulled down deep inside the meat while under the heat, rise back to the surface. This keeps the bite juicy and tender, and it is easy to work a knife through the meat. In the case of a stuffed roast, the resting time also seems to let the roast settle and enable a clean cut for serving, so stuffing doesn't come tumbling out under the knife.

Country Ribs with Black Cherry Red Wine Reduction and Gorgonzola

If you're familiar with the fare from the magazine *Taste of Home*, you'll realize that most of their recipes reside in the comfort food category. They seem to have their roots in church suppers and bring-a-dish family reunion concoctions germane to the South and Midwest. There's lots of Campbell's Soup, Tater Tots, Cool Whip, Velveeta, and other homey ingredients that take no more effort to work with than opening the can, bag, or box they came in. This isn't an insult. Indeed, there is something undeniably satisfying in the simplicity of such dishes. They fill both the soul and the belly, even if most don't appear on your cardiologist's list of recommended meals. While I often seek to create more complex dishes in the kitchen, when a guy's broken my heart or I'm feeling blue, I'm all for the Loaded Tater Tot casserole or a slow cooker full of creamy mac-n-cheese.

Of the types of these dishes that hail from the South, an ingredient you'll often find in preparing beef and pork is Coca-Cola or Dr. Pepper (oddly enough, Coke's competitor, Pepsi, is never used).

I was rarely allowed soda as a kid. Every time we asked for the treat, my mother recalled the time her childhood dentist put a pulled tooth in a glass of Coke, only to return the next week to find most of it eaten away. Coke's reputation for dissolving corrosion on car battery connection points is legendary, and I've heard you can clean a toilet, remove gum stuck to a shoe sole, and clean tile grout with it, among other uses. What that means to tough cuts of pork or beef is that Coke can help break down the thick, heavily used muscle fibers, collagen, and thick strands of connective tissue *while* imparting flavor at the same time.

Here's what you'll need for a nice dinner for two.

INGREDIENTS

Four thick country-style individual ribs
1 10-ounce bottle of black cherry soda
2 10-ounce packages of frozen black cherries
1 tablespoon of cinnamon
½ teaspoon of nutmeg

2 sprigs of fresh rosemary leaves*
2 cups of sweet red wine (a sweet Lambrusco or Grenache variety will work)**
¼ cup of organic table sugar
Crumbled Gorgonzola

INSTRUCTIONS

1. If you need to, thaw your ribs (page 40). Heat a large sauté pan to medium high. Lay the individual ribs on one of their wide sides in the pan, with ample room in between each rib. Leave the ribs alone on their first side down, sizzling away, for several minutes. They are ready to turn when you pick one up with a pair of tongs and they come away from the pan bottom cleanly and effortlessly. If they stick, leave them that side down until they don't stick. Once both wide sides are beautifully browned, stand the ribs on their fat side edge to brown, then on the rib curl side to brown again; lean the ribs against each other if need be to get them to stay upright. When all four sides are browned, set the ribs aside.

2. In a slow cooker (I use Breville's four-quart Risotto Plus Rice Cooker), pour in the bottle of black cherry soda (You can also use a can of Cherry Coke or other black cherry, and even Dr. Pepper or root beer). Add one bag of frozen black cherries and stir in the cinnamon, nutmeg, and rosemary leaves.

3. Pick up each of the ribs with tongs and set them on edge in the slow cooker basin so that at least part of all four are submerged. Leave for four hours on the low setting until the meat is separating from the bone, but still a tough enough to keep them together for a proper presentation. If the latter matters to you, knock 30 to 60 minutes off your cooking time.

4. When the ribs are almost done, start the cherry wine reduction. Put the wine and second bag of frozen cherries in a small sauce pan, bring to a low boil, and stir frequently until the sauce is reduced to a third and thickening. You can add the quarter-cup of sugar as I did, when I got impatient that the sauce was reducing but not thickening. Sprinkle in a bit of cinnamon and nutmeg if you wish. When you've gotten to the one-third reduction in volume, lid the pot and turn off the heat to let the sauce thicken before serving.

5. To serve, I cooked up a batch of pink rice. I laid two of the gorgeously cooked ribs over a cup of the rice and spooned over a generous ladle of cherries in their wine reduction sauce. I crumbled over some lovely Gorgonzola cheese as a counterpoint to the sweetness of the ribs and wine and cherry reduction. Elegant, eye-engaging on the plate, and beautiful in the mouth, this is a special-occasion dinner to put on your roster—or one to take the place of Wednesday night meatloaf and *make* the night special.

Crown Roast of Pork

Simpler than it looks! I don't usually tackle large pieces of meat unless I'm smoking something and using it in a variety of meals. For this recipe, I paid a visit to my butcher and ordered a full crown roast.

"You want a whole roast?" he asked, knowing I go it alone most of the time. "You know that's something like eight or nine pounds?"

"Yup," I answered, "I have a pan to fit it. . ."

I was extremely pleased to see that a crown roast of pork isn't nearly as expensive as a half standing rib roast of cow. My pork crown, at just under 10 pounds, cost about $56, while a seven-pound standing prime rib had cost me $90. It's a complete bargain—and let me tell you, 10 pounds of connected bone-in pork chops is a *lot* of meat. Sheesh, talk about leftovers when you're just a single girl!

So, what is a crown roast of pork? Really, it's a bone-in pork loin, the ribs Frenched (they've had the meat sleeved off them to leave them exposed), and the meat slightly split between the ribs to allow the rack (a full roast is a full rack of ribs) to be pulled into a circle and tied.

According to Google, a pig is supposed to have two sets of 14 ribs, but it also depends on the size and age of the pig. My roast had 16 ribs. You'll need a full rack to make the coveted circle, and it's not hard to do, but it's so much easier if your butcher has it Frenched, tied in a circle, and ready to go for you. This is purely for presentation and ooohs and ahhhs at the table, nothing else.

The essentials to getting a crown roast of pork on your table are the following:

* Have your butcher French the rib ends and tie the roast in a circle. There's no reason you should tussle with such a large piece of meat yourself to make it pretty. That's why you pay the guy in the white apron behind the counter.

* There's a lot of meat on a full crown roast. Be prepared to invite some friends.

- Be careful with your cooking reference books. While many volumes such as *Mastering the Art of French Cooking* are still invaluable tools, meat and crop production have changed substantially in many areas in the last 50-plus years. With those changes, so, too, have we adjusted our cooking temperatures and techniques.

- Leave the intimidation behind with this roast. Despite its terribly impressive finished looks, this is a cinch to put together.

My 9.95-pound roast came Frenched and tied from my butcher. I took a large, shallow roasting pan (an extra wide Calphalon), and swiped olive oil across the bottom. I set the roast in the pan and worked on something for the outside. Here's what you'll need:

INGREDIENTS

¼ cup fresh rosemary leaves

¼ cup fresh sage leaves

¼ cup rosemary infused olive oil

1 ½ teaspoons salt

1 teaspoon black pepper berries

1 ½ tablespoons crushed garlic

2 tablespoons Grey Poupon Mild and
     Creamy mustard

INSTRUCTIONS

1. Put all the ingredients in a food processor and combine. Note that pepper berries won't break down like they will when you run them in a spice or coffee grinder, but will split on the blades of your processor and release their flavors. There's not a lot of "dressing" for this recipe, about a ¾ cup, so don't worry if it doesn't look like it's enough. Take a spatula or your fingers and spread it inside and out of the crown circle, getting in between the ribs and definitely on the open face of the chops where they're tied together.

2. You can go stuffed or unstuffed with a crown roast, but I do think that stuffing's best left in a casserole dish on the side. Instead, I took two sweet onions, halved the smaller one lengthwise and the larger one in thirds, and wrapped the sections in bacon. I wedged three of these inside the circle, and placed the other three on top for grins.

3. Go low and slow: preheat the oven to a mere 250 degrees and slide the roast in. Leave the door closed for 2 ½ hours, though you can peek in once or twice to check on it. When a thermometer reads 145 degrees remove the roasting pan, tent the roast with foil, and turn the oven all the way up to 500 degrees while the roast sits outside.

4. After 30 minutes of pre-heating, put the roast back in for 20 minutes. There should be gorgeous coloring across the top three-quarters of the roast, with juices oozing. Remove the pan and set outside once more for 25 minutes, without tenting, before you begin to carve and serve.

5. This roast was *perfectly* done. I'm not a big pork chop fan (I prefer a prime rib of beef), but these thick, unbelievably juicy chops were an excellent meal. The light seasoning had been a smart choice and a little salt and pepper on the chop when it's served is all that is needed to bring out its full flavors. If you take on a big piece of meat for the first time and want to impress your guests, you cannot go wrong with this recipe.

Pork Loin Roast Stuffed with Roasted Red Peppers, Spinach, and Honeyed Chevre

In my experimentations in the kitchen, I've discovered that pork really does provide something almost intangible—a kind of sweetness, smoothness, silkiness, and better feel in the mouth—than the beef or veal or chicken or lamb for which I substituted it. (This is particularly true for ground pork, and I now won't even start a chili recipe with beef as a component.) Regardless, no matter where I worked it in, pork always seemed to improve the dish, sometimes greatly (chilis), sometimes subtly (the pork Bolognese sauce).

At the same time, pork has a list of other elements that go naturally with it: apples, cornbread, corn, rosemary, tomatoes, basil, and, of course, bacon. To that end I've tried to introduce new ways to work with these tried and true elements, giving you classic combinations in fresh ways ("Apple Scrapple Cinnamon Bread Pudding", page 113). This recipe is one such go, and I think it turned out beautifully. As you will see from the ingredient list, this is an uncomplicated recipe that is also not hard to assemble.

Here's what you'll need:

INGREDIENTS

1 3- to 4-pound pork loin roast, butterflied (and pounded for tenderness/thickness as necessary)
Salt and ground white pepper to taste
8 ounces of Honey Chevre (the Montchevre brand is fairly available)

1 tablespoon of butter
1 pound of fresh baby spinach
1 32-ounce jar of roasted red peppers
1 cup of honey, melted, plus another 2 tablespoons

INSTRUCTIONS

1. Have your butcher butterfly your pork loin roast (the full loin roast, *not* a tenderloin), and pound it out to a uniform thinness. If you have to do this yourself, see page 52.

2. Lay your butterflied pork loin roast, fat side down, on a clean, dry cutting board. Give it a light dose of salt and white ground pepper, then spread your honeyed goat cheese across the face of the roll, stopping short an inch on one end and two inches on the other.

3. In a large sauté pan, melt the tablespoon of butter and gently wilt your raw baby spinach in batches. You can wilt it all the way down to the stage where you'd make creamed spinach, but I prefer to wilt it about halfway there—you will still recognize the shape of the leaves, but a good portion of the water will be cooked out. As you finish each batch, use a slotted spoon to remove it from the pan and spread it out on the roast atop the chevre. Keep the pan warm while you complete the next step.

4. Drain the jar of roasted red peppers. You can roast your own, but the ones you get in a jar are wicked soft and have a little zip to them, thanks to the brine in which they're bottled. Take each wedge of pepper and lay on top of the spinach, laying the slices close together. There will be gaps, but try to minimize them so that you don't end up with a slice that has no pepper when you cut the finished roll for service.

5. Go back to the pan you used to wilt your spinach. The water should have evaporated by now, so add a bit more butter and 2 tablespoons of honey. Whisk it a bit until viscous, then drizzle half of it over the pepper sections.

6. Roll up your roast, starting with the end that has just one-inch of meat exposed and rolling towards the end with two inches exposed. Finish the roll and place it seam side down on your cutting board. Tie with kitchen twine at least three ties (middle and both ends), with two more as necessary for a particularly wide roast. The point is to make the roll as uniform from end to end as possible, without bulging in between the twine pieces, which will gap as they cook and spill out the stuffing, so if you need another piece or two of twine to make this happen, have at it. Rub the remaining salt and pepper thoroughly along the outside of the roast and set in a roasting rack over a roasting pan with a cup of water in it. Drizzle the remaining honey and butter over the length of the roast.

7. Preheat your oven to 450 degrees. Slide the pan with the roast above it in for 15 minutes, then drop the temperature back to 350 and go for about an hour. The roast should brown nicely after that initial high temperature toast. If it's getting too brown but isn't cooked yet, tent it with foil and check every 10 minutes until done. To determine doneness, insert a probe thermometer into the meat (not the stuffing) and it should register about 150. Some say 160, but I think that dries out the pork. I actually prefer about 145, as this roast will continue to cook a little when out of the oven. Remove the roast and sit for 15 to 20 minutes under a foil tent.

8. This is so pretty when sliced. It has the classic Italian flag colors, but the flavors, piqued by the sweet goat cheese and the extra drizzled honey, will take your taste buds somewhere else—and it will be a glorious, delicious place indeed. Choose a Sancerre Sauvignon Blanc to go with this, one that's a little fruity and sweet, but not super high on the acid side.

Roast Pork Loin Tortilla Soup

Skimming through Pinterest one day, I noticed half a dozen or more different recipes for chicken tortilla soup. That got me to thinking that a roast pork variation would be a perfect addition to this book.

Now, you might ask: why bother roasting the pork at all? I really wanted that roast pork taste to shine through. You could certainly take the fat cap off a raw roast and do the elbow work of cutting the raw meat into bite-sized chunks, allowing it to cook in the stew from start to finish; however, it won't have any depth or real flavor to it. The simple combination of salt and pepper and a short hot bake followed by a longer, slower roast brings out all those flavors.

There's another reason to do this, and it has to do with texture. By roasting, the slight under-doneness allows you to slice the loin super-thin before adding it to soup. This provides a very tender bite in the finished product.

Here's what you'll need.

INGREDIENTS

1 2- to 3-pound boneless pork loin roast
Salt and pepper to taste
2 pints of cherry tomatoes
2 tablespoons of crushed garlic
1 12-ounce jar of Goya tomato sofrito
4 cups of chicken stock
1 ½ to 2 cups of cooked black beans
    (one to two 16-ounce cans)
2 4-ounce cans of diced green chilis
1 tablespoon of cumin (or more to taste)

1 tablespoon of chili powder (or more to taste)
2 teaspoons of garlic powder
2 teaspoons of hot smoked paprika
2 teaspoons of Mexican oregano
1 16-ounce jar of red enchilada sauce
1 large bunch of fresh cilantro
Juice from one lime
Plain or lime tortilla chips or salted and baked
    tortilla strips
Water as needed

1. Rub your roast with coarsely ground sea salt and cracked black pepper. You want the flavor of nothing but roasted pork to come through.

2. Preheat your oven to 425. Set the roast, with the fat cap on the top, in the roasting rack (one usually reserved for chickens) over a large roasting pan that contains a cup or so of water. Keep the roast in the oven for 15 to 20 minutes or until the meat starts to brown and the fat sizzles, then lower the oven to 325 and continue to cook for no more than 30 minutes for a two-pound roast. Go another 15 to 20 for a roast in the three-pound range.

3. This roast will be a little undercooked, but not by a lot. Pink in the middle is just fine, as the pork will continue cooking in the soup. If you want to verify where the cooking stage is with a probe thermometer, get your internal temp to 135 instead of the normal 145, then take it out of the oven, cover lightly with aluminum foil, and let it come to a temperature where you can handle it with your fingers.

4. While the pork is cooking, start on the soup foundation. Take two pints of sweet cherry tomatoes, spread them in a single layer in the bottom of a small casserole, then drizzled with olive oil and sprinkled with sea salt. Roast them in the oven in a rack under the pork. When you are ready to pull the roast out, the tomatoes should be burst open and sizzling.

5. About 20 minutes before the pork and tomatoes are done, warm up a tablespoon or three of olive oil in the bottom of a stock pot, the temperature on medium low, and sweat the crushed garlic until light brown so it releases its sweetness. Add the sofrito and hot tomatoes, including their rendered juices and olive oil.

6. Next, deglaze the roasting pan, using a cup or so of chicken stock and making sure to scrape all the good roasted bits off the bottom of the pan. Add this deeply flavored liquid to the stock pot and raise the temperature a little, stirring occasionally until the mixture is gently bubbling.

7. Add the beans, green chilies, spices, and enchilada sauce. Bring the pot up again to a low bubble, stirring occasionally, then add three cups of chicken stock.

8. Slice your rested pork roast very thin or medium-thin using a serrated bread knife. Once you have the roast sliced, cut each slice into strips, adding two to three cups to the soup (leftover pork can be reserved for a quick toss in the frying pan to make a hot sandwich). Add more stock as you need; you don't want the liquid to be broth thin, but neither do you want it to be stew thick. Bring the pot to a rolling boil, lid the pot, and reduce the flame to low.

9. Add a large bunch of chopped cilantro and a tablespoon or so of lime juice to the soup. Taste and add salt and lime juice as needed, then keep the pot covered on low for at least an hour to let the flavors meld. I actually let soups like this simmer on very low heat through the afternoon and mid-evening, then leave them to sit on the stove overnight on a cold burner before being refrigerated the next morning and brought back to life for lunch or dinner.

10. To serve, place broken tortilla chips in the bottom of a soup bowl and ladle the hot soup on top. Sprinkle a few more tortilla chips on top or multicolored salad topper tortilla strips. If you're not a tortilla chip person, go with Fritos. Other additions can be a can of hominy (which adds yet another textural element to this soup) or a cup of roasted corn. No matter which way you go, this is a flavor-packed, richly textured soup for which you'll be entirely happy you substituted pork for the usual chicken.

Roasted Pork Tenderloin Chili

When making chili in all its many variations—except for turkey chili and "vegetarian" chili, both of which should be outlawed—the most important thing to get right is the bite of the meat. Ground meat is undoubtedly the most common form: Use a good 80/20 mix of ground chuck, drain the fat, and add the rest that makes the chili sing. A couple years ago I started going half and half ground chuck and fresh ground pork, but I've now stopped using ground beef altogether and gone straight pork. It's not that I don't like chili made with ground beef, it's just that chili with ground pork is, well, better.

My red chilies are always super-thick, stand-a-spoon-in-'em affairs with very little sauce or liquid. But when I decided to go with roast pork tenderloin instead of ground pork, I thought a chili with more viscosity would better highlight the bite of the tenderloin—and I was right.

Here's what you'll need.

INGREDIENTS

3 pounds of pork tenderloin (usually come in a two-pack)
4 tablespoons of ground cumin
3 tablespoons of chili powder
3 teaspoons of cayenne pepper
2 teaspoon of smoked paprika
1 ½ tablespoons of onion powder
1 ½ tablespoon of garlic powder
1 ½ teaspoons of crushed red pepper flakes
2 tablespoons of light brown sugar
Salt and pepper to taste
Olive oil

2 tablespoons of crushed garlic
1 large onion, rough chopped
1 32-ounce can of crushed tomatoes
1 32-ounce can of whole peeled tomatoes
1 16-ounce jar of Mrs. Renfro's Salsa (hot, medium, or mild)
1 16-ounce can of black beans
1 cup of Zinfandel wine
½ cup of peanut butter (smooth; *not* organic or all-natural)
1 large bunch of fresh cilantro

1. Make a rub for your pork tenderloin. Combine one tablespoon of cumin; one teaspoon each of chili powder, cayenne, and smoked paprika; and a half-teaspoon each of onion powder, garlic powder, and red pepper flakes. To this, add brown sugar and a teaspoon of sea salt and cracked black pepper. Combine with a fork until well mixed and the ingredients are evenly distributed.

2. Pour half the rub mixture over each tenderloin (there's usually a pair in the average three-pound package) and rub it all over the meat with your hands, making sure the entire surface and the ends are coated. Place the loins in an appropriately sized, low-side casserole, gratin, or roasting pan and slide into a preheated 400-degree oven for 20 to 25 minutes. To determine doneness, it should be prettily colored on the outside, but not overly dark brown. A finished internal temperature taken with a probe thermometer should be about 145, but it's okay to undercook this a bit as it will finish cooking in the chili; I suggest getting the probe thermometer to 135. Remove from the oven, tent with foil, and let them come to room temperature.

3. While the tenderloins are cooling, start the chili foundation. In a large stockpot, warm olive oil on medium-low heat. Add chopped garlic and slowly sauté until golden brown. Add chopped onion and sauté until translucent, then add crushed tomatoes and whole peeled tomatoes, as well as the jar of salsa and black beans (include the liquid from the can of beans, as it will help thicken the chili). Stir in the rest of the spices, lid the pot, and gradually bring to a low bubble, stirring occasionally.

4. While the chili foundation is coming together, dice the cooled pork tenderloin into ¾-inch chunks. Add the tenderloin to the pot. Deglaze the tenderloin's roasting pan with the cup of Zinfandel, reducing to about a half-cup, then add that to the chili, too. Bring the chili to a happy but not overly aggressive boil, lid on and stirring from time to time. Add peanut butter and swirl it around to melt and combine.* Reduce the pot to low and simmer for an hour or two (though longer over low heat won't hurt), or transfer to a slow cooker set on low for the afternoon. Give it a swirl from time to time to make sure nothing's sticking to the bottom.

5. An hour before serving, rough chop your fresh cilantro, including the stems, and stir it into the chili. Fifteen minutes before serving, bring it up to that happy bubbling state again and serve promptly.

6. The roasted pork tenderloin introduces a distinct difference in taste and texture to the chili compared to more traditional recipes that use other ground meats. As this chili has a good amount of V8-thick liquid, it is superb over rice, pasta, a sweet hunk of cornbread, ciabatta bread, or even a toasted English muffin to mop up the excess liquid goodness. Oddly enough, while I like Fritos as a topping for my chili from time to time, they didn't do well in this iteration, since this more viscous variation turned the chips into an unpleasant, soppy mess.

*TIP I had the distinct privilege of getting to know the award-winning Texas Tex-Mex chef Matt Martinez, when I lived in San Antonio. He regrettably passed several years ago (his son Matt Martinez III now runs the renowned Matt's Rancho Martinez restaurants in the Dallas, Texas, area), but, when he was alive, we had a conversation about chili once. One of the keys to good chili that he passed on to me was adding peanut butter. I tried it, and he was right. No matter how spicy, no matter how mild, no matter pork, beef, or chicken based, peanut butter does something that brings all the riots of flavors together into harmony, yet without diluting any of them. And while you can catch the aroma of warm peanut butter as it cooks in, you can't really taste the peanut butter once the dish is finished. Now, I always add peanut butter to my chilis (and sometimes other dishes, like tomato bisque), but I've learned a couple things along the way.

First, add peanut butter like you add salt and pepper, a little at a time. I start with a half-cup, but I've gone as large as two, depending in the size of the pot of chili I'm cooking and the intensity of the pepper level. Second, go with a straight-up commercial brand like Skippy or Peter Pan. I have tried repeatedly to use organic and all-natural peanut butters and been very disappointed with the results. The organics fail to melt and distribute, and you always end up with a glob of grainy peanut butter on your spoon. The all-naturals also tend to not distribute well, leaving streaks of PB here and there. If the flame is too high on the pot, you'll also end up with burnt peanut butter in the bottom of the pot. Stick with commercial creamy peanut butters, which will produce the harmonizing effect you desire.

CHAPTER 2
PORK SHOULDER

Barbecued Pulled Pork Mac-N-Cheese

Is there anyone who doesn't like macaroni-and-cheese? One of my many cookbooks is devoted solely to this ultimate comfort food and I use it often when I have time to cook and feel like spending $50 on cheese. Unfortunately, I don't always have a the time or enough $50 bills, so when I ran across a recipe for making macaroni-and-cheese in the slow cooker, I thought, *What the hell, let's give this a try.*

There really isn't anything to making mac-n-cheese in a slow cooker. What I did was layer the ingredients in my slow cooker, a four-quart model from Breville. One of the few problems I have with making mac-n-cheese in the slow cooker is that the dried pasta takes up so much room, and because it is inflexible, it's difficult to incorporate your ingredients until the dish is nearly cooked. Yes, there are slow cooker recipes that tell you to cook your pasta separately first, but that kind of nullifies the beauty of using only the slow cooker to cook everything. By putting dry pasta in the slow cooker, you end up with a more al dente bite, and with half the mess. I've been pleasantly surprised by the results, and, frankly, I find that mac-n-cheese made this way reheats better for leftovers.

Recently I came across an idea for mac-n-cheese that called for barbecue sauce. That got me thinking about a good hamburger loaded with barbecue sauce and sharp cheddar cheese. And *that* got me thinking about this recipe. Here's what you'll need:

INGREDIENTS

1 18-ounce bottle of spicy barbecue sauce (I used Stubbs' All-Natural Spicy)
1 8-ounce package of cream cheese, room temperature
3 cups of cooked pulled pork

4 cups of extra sharp white or yellow cheddar cheese
16 ounces of dried gemelli pasta
1 cup of water

1. Prepare your pulled pork in a slow cooker (see page 18–19). I usually start with an eight-pound, bone-in shoulder roast and cook for about 12 hours (with leftovers). The only drawback with the slow cooker is that you don't get any browning on the outside like you would with a smoker or the oven. An easy solution to introducing color to the pork is with a fry pan. Give your pulled pork a rough chop and put in a skillet on medium-high, letting it sizzle for a couple minutes. Once they're crisping up, flip the pieces over with a spatula and treat the other side the same. Not only will you brown the pork, but you will also impart better flavors.

2. Put a third of the bottle of barbecue sauce in the bottom of the pot. Try to use a spicier barbecue sauce rather than a super-sweet brew, which can produce an overly cloying taste.

3. On top of the sauce, layer on half the pulled pork. Make sure your pulled pork is trimmed of the heaviest fat pieces and either hand-pulled or chopped into decent fork-sized pieces.

4. Chunk up your cream cheese and layer on top of the pork. Add half the shredded cheese, then the dry pasta. I chose gemelli, a twined dual-strand stick pasta that would work on the fork with the pulled pork, as opposed to a pasta type that holds a lot of sauce, like a shell; this isn't an ooey-gooey mac-n-cheese.

5. Top the dried pasta with the rest of the pork, pour over the remainder of the barbecue sauce, and top with the other half of the shredded cheese. Lid the slow cooker and set it on high.

6. I made this batch at lunch and it was mostly finished when I got home at five. I gave it a good stir to mix it all up and evenly incorporate the melted cream cheese and cheddar. I added about a cup of water, put the lid back on, and reduced the slow cooker to its low setting. One hour later, I popped a cold beer and spooned up a generous serving of this different and decadent mac-n-cheese.

TIP This was actually better as leftovers. After that first dinner, I stuck the remainder in the fridge. A couple nights later, I spooned a dinner helping into a gratin dish, sprinkled over a little water, covered the dish in foil, then popped it in my toaster oven for 45 minutes at 350 degrees. It was fantastic, even better than the first night's serving. The flavors were better married, and that little bit of steaming in the toaster oven helped "re-sauce" the dish.

This re-saucing is, in fact, one of the reasons I've begun cooking more mac-n-cheese in the slow cooker. Slow-cooker mac-n-cheese reheated this way—sprinkle of water, foil—returns the dish to its original state, something that doesn't seem to happen with the more time-consuming, sauce-from-scratch, stove-top to oven baked mac-n-cheese recipes. Leftovers from those more intense recipes always seem to separate upon reheating, especially those that use butter—and the pasta tends to get gummy.

Bottom line: give the slow-cooker a whirl when that comfort food urge strikes. You won't be sorry.

Better-Than-Bar Nachos

Ever get a craving for bar food? Of course you do, everyone does. My go-to pub dish is a plate of nachos. They rank a perfect 10 on the scale of things easy to make—there isn't anywhere near the mess that comes from deep-frying foods, and you can make nachos about as many different ways as you can soup.

While I like the standard nacho arrangement just fine—tortilla chips, ground beef, cheese, and jalapeños topped with guacamole and sour cream—that stack gets a little redundant. Also, you can never tell when you slice into a jalapeño just how hot it is, and I hate it when a jalapeño takes over and silences all the other flavors in a plate of nachos. All that said, here's a rendition that I think truly elevates this icon of bar food, while making great use of leftover pulled pork. Here's what you'll need:

INGREDIENTS

3 cups of pulled pork

1 16-ounce can of refried beans

2 cups of very sharp white cheddar cheese

½ cup of chopped white or yellow onion

½ cup of chopped peppadew peppers*

1 full-size bag of Doritos Nacho Cheese

1 16-ounce jar of medium-hot green salsa

*TIP Peppadews are a semi-sweet, round little pepper, a little smaller than a jawbreaker gumball. They come from the Limpopo province of South Africa, which makes them decidedly different and a little exotic. They are also delicious. Usually sold pickled, they're a little zesty, a little sweet, and juicily tender—altogether a wonderful change from jalapeños, habaneros, and the like.

1. Prepare your pulled pork in a slow cooker (see page 18–19). I usually start with an eight-pound, bone-in shoulder roast and cook for about 12 hours (with leftovers). The only drawback with the slow cooker is that you don't get any browning on the outside like you would with a smoker or the oven. An easy solution to introducing color to the pork is with a fry pan. Give your pulled pork a rough chop and put in a skillet on medium-high, letting it sizzle for a couple minutes. Once they're crisping up, flip the pieces over with a spatula and treat the other side the same. Not only will you brown the pork, but you will also impart better flavors.

2. While the pork is frying, heat the refried beans in a small saucepan and add water to thin them. Shred your cheese. Give the onion and peppadews a rough chop.

3. Build the nachos. On a large oven-proof plate or a low-sided gratin dish, spread a generous and deep layer of Doritos. Depth is important since Doritos don't hold up as well as regular tortilla chips when they're paired with wet ingredients in a hot oven, so a deep first layer will provide you with some chips that are still whole, and with a crunch to them.

4. Add half your pork and half the onions to this first layer of chips. Sprinkle on half the cheese, then drizzle over most of the refried beans. Don't overdo the beans, or you'll turn your Doritos to mush. Add a second deep layer of chips, the other half of the pork, the peppadews, the second half of the cheese, and drizzle over your salsa.

5. Pop the whole thing into a preheated 350-degree oven for about 20 minutes, then finish them off under the broiler for three or four minutes. Serve the whole thing up with extra fresh and crisp Doritos and a couple cold beers for a nacho plate that'll beat anything your local dive bar has to offer.

Better-Than-Takeout Eggrolls, with Four Variations

Unless you were raised in an Asian household with traditional Asian foods, it's hard to whip up those dishes that come easily in handy takeout boxes. Things like fish, plum, black bean, hoisin, and myriad other sauces unique to Chinese fare (at least "Chinese" as we know it here in the US) don't appear in any other dishes of non-Asian origin. The ingredients behind them are often difficult to identify; even the traditional Chinese five-spice mix has a flavor profile unique among spice mixes. (For the record, most are made of blend of cinnamon, cloves, fennel, star anise, and Szechuan peppercorns, though some also include ginger, nutmeg, and licorice, which would make them six-, seven-, and eight-spice mixes—but I digress.)

I dabble with Chinese and Thai recipes from time to time. Stir-frys are actually easy when you have a good cookbook, an excellent wok, access to *all* the ingredients (what are you going to substitute for fish sauce?). Understand that it goes *fast*, so you have to have all your ingredients chopped and ready to go—totally unlike most of the cooking I do because, let's face it, I'm a low and slow kind of girl.

Among the recipes that require strict adherence to ingredients, their quantities, and their preparation, there are a couple of Asian take-out items you can make freestyle and without a lot of fuss—and you should therefore not be intimidated into dialing the phone and ordering a #6, a #21, and a bag full of wontons and fortune cookies instead of making your own eggrolls. Here's what you'll need for a rather traditional Chinese take-out version. Since egg rolls are all about what you put inside them like burritos and pizza, here are some variations.

Each recipe makes six to eight eggrolls.

TRADITIONAL CHINESE TAKE-OUT EGGROLLS

1 cup of chopped pulled pork or browned ground pork
1 teaspoon of chopped fresh garlic
1 teaspoon of ginger
1 teaspoon of sugar
2 tablespoons of soy sauce
1 teaspoon of sesame oil
½ cup of shredded broccoli and carrots
½ cup of finely chopped cabbage (green or red)
3 to 4 finely chopped green onions, greens and whites
Eggroll/wonton wrappers (square-shaped)
Optional: Crushed red chili flakes

INSTRUCTIONS

1. Prepare the pork. If using pulled pork (page 17–21), chop fairly finely and sauté briefly in a high heat pan with garlic, ginger, sugar, and soy sauce until heated through and the meat has a little sauce to it. Remove and place in a medium bowl. If using ground pork, sauté the meat in the pan alone, drain off the excess fat, then finish browning with garlic, ginger, sugar, and soy sauce.

2. In a clean saute pan on high heat, warm the sesame oil and toss in the shredded broccoli and carrots (you can buy this combo already shredded in most grocery stores). Stir vigorously, but lid the pan in between stirrings to help steam the vegetables. They should be brightly colored and close to tender when finished.

3. Add the cooked vegetables to the bowl with the hot pork. Add in the finely chopped cabbage and green onions and toss to combine. If you want to make these a little spicy, add in a shake or two of crushed red chili flakes.

SOUTHWESTERN EGGROLLS

1 cup of chopped pulled pork or ground pork
1 tablespoon of cumin
1 tablespoon of chili powder
1 small can of chopped green chilis
1 cup of whole black beans, drained
1 cup of shredded queso fresco or Monterey Jack cheese
1 cup of finely minced fresh cilantro
Eggroll/wonton wrappers (square-shaped)
Alternative version:
Substitute one cup of pico de gallo for the cheese

INSTRUCTIONS

1. Prepare the pork. For pulled pork (page 17–21), crisp it up a bit in a sauté pan, tossing in the cumin and chili powder at the finish. Remove to a medium mixing bowl when done. For ground pork, sauté until cooked through, drain off the excess fat, then toss in the spices and cook a couple minutes more before removing to the mixing bowl.

2. Add the rest of the ingredients to the pork and toss to combine evenly.

PIZZA EGGROLLS

1 cup of Italian sausage
1 teaspoon of garlic
1 teaspoon of dried oregano
1 cup of finely minced basil leaves
1 cup of shredded mozzarella
½ cup of marinara sauce
Eggroll/wonton wrappers (square-shaped)
Alternate version
Substitute finely chopped pepperoni for the Italian sausage

1. If using Italian sausage (loose meat, not links), sauté in a hot pan until almost cooked through. Make sure to break the sausage down to fine pieces, rather than chunks, as you go. Drain off the excess fat and finish cooking the sausage with the garlic and oregano, a couple minutes, then remove to a medium mixing bowl. Note: If you've been unable to reduce the size of the sausage to a grind, pulse it a couple times in a food processor.

2. Add the remaining ingredients to the sausage and combine until evenly distributed.

SPAGHETTI EGG ROLLS

1 cup of Italian sausage
1 tablespoon of olive oil
½ cup of finely chopped red peppers
½ cup of finely chopped green peppers
¼ cup of finely chopped onion
1 teaspoon of oregano
1 tablespoon of chopped garlic
¾ cup of cooked fettuccini noodles
½ cup of your favorite tomato sauce
Eggroll/wonton wrappers (square-shaped)

INSTRUCTIONS

1. Saute the Italian sausage until cooked through, breaking it down to a small crumble as you go. Drain off the excess fat and put the meat in a medium mixing bowl. If you are unable to break down the sausage to a fine grind in the pan, drain the fat off and pulse the sausage a couple times in a food processor to break down.

2. Using the same pan in which you cooked the sausage, heat the olive oil and add the peppers, onion, oregano, and garlic. Saute until the onions are translucent and add the vegetable mix to the sausage in the mixing bowl.

3. Cook your pasta. Bring medium pot of water with some olive oil and salt to boil. Grab a stack of the noodles, probably the diameter of a nickel in your grasp, and break the noodles in half. Add to the boiling water and cook until just past al dente. Drain and immediately add to the sausage and vegetables, then the sauce, and toss to combine.

ASSEMBLING THE EGGROLLS

This isn't any harder than rolling a sandwich wrap or making a burrito, but you do have to use a bit more finesse and go about the process gently. Eggroll or wonton wrappers are more delicate than a tortilla, though that doesn't mean you have to treat them daintily. In fact, they can actually be easier to work with than tortillas. Where you'll run into problems is with tearing at the edges on the ends and with the insides poking through.

The solution to both issues lies in being conservative with the amount of filling you use. This is also why you sauté vegetables, so that they are softened a bit and, thus, will resist punching through the wonton wrapper from the inside. I would even tell you to let your shredded cheeses come to room temperature, thus making the shredded pieces more flexible.

One more note about these fillings. I was deliberately careful with the amount of wet ingredients like marinara sauce and mustard. You do not want your fillings to be a soggy wet mess that will soak through the eggroll wrappers. What you want is just enough of the wet ingredients to coat the other ingredients and add flavor and richness. If you need more than the amount recommended here, go ahead, but don't let your fillings get to a drippy, blue-plate special egg salad consistency.

1. To assemble, take a wonton wrapper and lay it on a cutting board with an end pointed toward you. Have a small bowl of water on hand.

2. Place 1 ½ to 2 serving spoon helpings of filling in the center of the wrapper and horizontal to you—bisecting the diamond from one pointed end across to the other pointed end. Do *not* spread out the filling. You want to have at least an 1 ½ inches of exposed wonton wrapper at each end, and plenty of space around the top and bottom to make the roll.

3. Dip your index finger in water and run it down each edge of the wrapper. Take the end of the wrapper pointing toward you and bring it up over the center of the filling. Do the same with each end, pressing down on the wet edges to help them seal against each other. With these three points folded in, roll the eggroll forward (away from you) until the roll is wholly formed. Run your finger over the seam, using more water if necessary, and set seam-side down on a plate for deep-frying or on a cookie sheet or jellyroll pan lined with parchment paper.

COOKING THE EGGROLLS

For Frying—Heat a quantity of oil (peanut or canola oil) in a deep-sided sauté pan to 375. You'll need enough oil to come about halfway up the rolls. Cook in batches of two or three eggrolls at a time, turning when the downside is toasty brown to finish the other side the same way. You'll want to cook in batches, because every time you add food to hot oil, the oil temperature drops. Get it too low and the oil will struggle to return to the proper temperature, leaving you with grease-soaked eggrolls for a finished product, because they will have taken much longer to cook. Hot and fast is the rule for deep-frying.

For Baking—I find I get damn near the same "take-out" eggroll experience when baking them as I do with frying them, but with about half the mess and hassle. To bake, preheat your oven to 400 degrees. Brush each eggroll with melted duck fat or bacon grease—even a little bit of melted butter will work. Don't slather any of these on, just give them a gentle brushing with a bristle pastry brush. Make sure the eggrolls have space between them on the pan. Into the oven they go for 15 minutes or so, until they are the same golden brown you'd expect from a deep-fried version.

TO SERVE

Hard to have an eggroll and not want to dip it in something. Try the following for the recipes above.

- Traditional Chinese Eggrolls—any number of the bottled sauces from brands like Thai Kitchen (red chili and ginger, pineapple and chili, sweet and sour), traditional duck sauce and Chinese hot mustard, or wasabi mayonnaise.

- Southwestern Eggrolls—red or green salsa are natural choices, especially when heated, but also try warming up some enchilada sauce. Sour cream and guacamole are no-brainers, and ranch dressing rocks.

- Pizza Eggrolls—go for piping hot marinara sauce or pesto.

- Spaghetti Eggrolls—any hot marinara, tomato and garlic, or pesto will work just as well here as it does with the pizza eggrolls, but if you really want to add some pizazz, heat up some Alfredo sauce for dipping or spoon on some black olive tapenade.

Pulled Pork Breakfast Scramble

If you flip through the pages of this book, you'll notice that a lot of the recipes derive from one source, either slices or pulled meat taken from a smoked or slow-roasted Boston butt. There are also several recipes derived from pork loin or tenderloin. The reason for this is pretty simple—I live by myself, and these are large cuts of meat. Once I get beyond the ham dinner or pulled pork barbeque sandwich, I have a *lot* of meat left over. Some say necessity is the mother of invention. I say it's leftover pork. Here's what you'll need for this awesome breakfast dish.

INGREDIENTS

3 cups of pulled/shredded Boston butt

2 tablespoons of bacon fat

2 bunches of green onions (8 to 10 onions, chopped, whites and greens included)

2 cups of cooked jasmine rice

6 jumbo eggs

1 cup of whole milk

2 tablespoons of melted butter

Salt and pepper to taste

1 teaspoon of cayenne pepper

INSTRUCTIONS

There are a thousand ways to cook a Boston butt. I always opt for smoking, but when I moved to Connecticut in 2014, the house I leased had no outside electrical outlets. Since both my smokers are electric, that relegates my smoking to the warm months when I can run a long extension cord through an open window or door. No can do in December, so I started experimenting with the slow cooker. I use the large All-Clad with the non-stick insert that can also be set on a burner and sear a piece of meat.

1. Beyond your chosen method—smoke, oven, or slow cooker—fix your Boston butt the way you like it (page 17–21). Inject it, rub it, kiss it goodnight, do whatever you like to flavor it, then cook it low and slow and long so that you end up with finger-licking good pulled pork that shreds away from the bone. The only caveat I would give you for this recipe is that you want pork that isn't wearing sauce or a lot of sweet, sugar-based rub. Use shredded pork closer to the bone or pork that's had a good spicy dry rub applied.

2. When the pulled pork is ready (fork-size chunks, if you would), heat up a large sauté pan and melt bacon fat over medium to medium-high heat. Add pulled pork in a single, even layer across the pan bottom when the bacon fat is hot enough to make the pork sizzle. Lower the heat just a bit after a couple minutes, letting the pork get crusty on the bottom before flipping it (in several turns) with a spatula to crisp up the other side a bit. Add the chopped green onions (should be about a cup and a half) and mix in with the browning pork.

3. Add rice on top of the pork and onions but don't mix it in yet. You can use either freshly made rice for this or leftover rice from the night before. If using leftover cold rice, be sure to break it up so it's not all in one clump, and sprinkle on a bit of water. Lid the pan and turn the heat down to just below medium. What you're doing now is rehydrating the rice by steaming it, while reducing how much you're cooking the pork and onions.

4. Once the lid is on the pan, whisk the eggs with the milk and melted butter. Give the lidded pan five to seven minutes, then check the rice. If it distributes easily (individual grains rather than lumps and clumps), mix it into the pork and onions, then pour your egg mixture over the top of all of it.

5. Let the eggs sit there and cook slowly for a bit, three to five minutes, depending on the size of your pan and the heat level on your burner. This is a good time to sprinkle on some salt, black pepper, and a pinch of cayenne if you're so inclined.

6. Once your eggs are starting to set—you should see the edges contract slightly away from the side of the pan, but don't let this get anywhere near a solid, frittata-like state—go ahead and take a flat-edged wooden spoon and gently start to turn the mixture. I say gently, because you really want this to stay light and fluffy, one of the reasons you put milk in the eggs. If you get too aggressive with your stirring, you might end up with a muddied mess. Stir a little, then let it cook some more before stirring again. Constant stirring breaks apart the egg too much, which will cause the egg to lose its smooth texture.*

7. This really isn't a complicated dish. It took me longer to type this out than it did to cook it. It's simple meals like this that can really start the day right. I ate it just as it was, scooped up with warm flour tortillas. On another morning I added a couple slices of fresh avocado and yet another dollop of sour cream. You could add salsa, cheese, or even refried beans, but don't overdo it. This is good plain as it is.

---

*TIP   If you're cooking for a crowd and using a larger pan for this, your edges will cook faster than the center. After two or three easy stirs, about two-thirds of the egg will be cooked, with the center still fairly wet looking. At this point, take your spatula and lift up on one edge to fold roughly half of the mix over the other. This way, the more cooked outside will sandwich the slightly undercooked middle, allowing the egg to remain fluffy as it finishes cooking.

Pulled Pork Sandwich with Apple, Pecan, and Red Cabbage Slaw

I learned about pulled pork in Virginia, where I lived for 25 years before a variety of career moves saw me restlessly wandering the country. I had never really been a big fan of barbecue—the eating with hands, messy and sticky faces and hands—but when I started to hunt, that changed.

In Virginia, the first Monday closest to Labor Day has long been the opening day of mourning dove season. Now, in Virginia, that's usually a hot, muggy day no different than any of the other hot, muggy days of summer in the South on the East Coast. There's often not a lot of shooting to be done, too hot for even the birds to move before dusk and the end of legal shooting light, but no one cares. There's pulled pork to be had.

The men who run the giant, old oil barrel pit have been up since the wee hours of the morning, getting the fire hot, splitting a freshly killed hog, and splaying it on the grill for a long, slow, succulent cook. When the shooting's done or the end of legal shooting light arrives, the line to the gorgeous, sacrificed pig is deep.

This kind of pig, so good you want to go home with a belly aching from overeating, is traditionally served on soft white hamburger rolls, often with a spoonful of baked beans and another of traditional carrot and green cabbage coleslaw, and then a splash of the red pepper flake and vinegar-based sauce that region's barbecue is known for.

I do love that sandwich combination, but since I make my smoked pork shoulders a dozen different ways, I've found mixing up the slaw can really enhance this terrific meal. This one here has become my favorite for a smoked pork done with a sweet rub, rather than a spicy rub.

Here's what you'll need for a half-dozen sandwiches:

INGREDIENTS

6 cups of hot pulled pork

1 ½ cups of pecan halves, rough chopped

4 cups of finely shredded crisp red cabbage

2 Granny Smith apples, peeled, cored, and rough chopped

¼ cup of mayonnaise

2 tablespoons of apple cider vinegar

2 tablespoons of light brown sugar

6 oversized hamburger rolls, soft Kaiser rolls, or soft eight-inch sub rolls

INSTRUCTIONS

1. Prepare your pulled pork (page 17–21).

2. The only cooking you need do for this recipe, besides the pork shoulder itself, is the toasting of the pecans. Warm a saute pan to medium heat, toss in your pecans in a single layer, and toast them, stirring or flipping them in the pan occasionally, until they barely start to turn a more golden brown and smell heavenly.

3. In a mixing bowl, mix the cabbage, apples, mayonnaise, cider vinegar, and sugar. Toss to combine, then add in your hot pecans and toss one more time.

4. Split your bread, pile on a cup of hot pulled pork, then a generous helping of this awesome slaw, and sit back and enjoy.

Pulled Pork, Butternut Squash, and Sugar Snap Peas in Tarragon Cream Sauce

As I've noted in several places, it's hard to make pulled pork without making a lot of it. Most Boston butts—the cut I use most frequently—run in the seven to nine pound range boneless, heavier with the bone in. That's a pile of meat, and that leaves me with lots of leftovers.

One of the last smokes I did in 2014, before the chill set in and prevented me from using my electric smokers outside the house, coincided with the abundance of butternut squash arriving at the market. Truly, I couldn't get away from the stuff, so in the spirit of if-you-can't-beat-'em-join-'em, I caved and bought two. Here's what I came up with in this savory, terrifically fragrant recipe.

INGREDIENTS

3 to 4 cups of butternut squash, chopped in one-inch cubes

4 cups of pulled pork, preferably one that had a light and sweet rub (no barbecue sauce)

½ teaspoon of salt

½ teaspoon of white pepper

2 teaspoons of dried tarragon

2 cups of sweet sugar snap peas

2 tablespoons of butter

2 cups of white wine

2 shallots, finely minced

Leaves from two to three sprigs of fresh tarragon

1 cup of heavy cream

INSTRUCTIONS

1. Cook your butternut squash first. One good-sized squash will yield enough for this dish. Cut the squash in half along its length. Place each half cut side down in a shallow roasting pan, pour in a couple cups of water (so it comes up the sides of the squash a bit), and bake in a preheated 375-degree oven for about 90 minutes. You want to be able to easily push a fork into it, but it should still have some firmness so it can be cut into chunks. Test with a fork at the 60-minute mark to get an idea for how much longer you have to go, then every 10 or 15 minutes until done. Add a cup of water as needed if the pan is about to go dry during the bake. Once the squash is cooked, remove the squash to a plate and set on the counter to cool.

2. Once again, this is a recipe that works off leftovers from a smoked or slow-roasted Boston butt or picnic. If you don't have leftovers, quickly roast a couple of pork tenderloins and cut them up. You could even use a mild ham. No matter what you use, and especially if you use pulled pork, take a sharp kitchen knife and give your hunk of meat a rough chop so that your meat pieces are of a uniform size that work nicely on a fork.

3. Turn back to your cooled butternut squash. Taking a small spoon, gently scrape out the seeds and dispose. Then, with a sharp paring knife, carefully peel away the squash's skin. Now you should be able to cut your squash. Do so in one-inch chunks and put in a mixing bowl, tossing with a little bit of salt, white pepper, and the ground dried tarragon. Add in your chopped pork.

4. Next, blanch the sugar snap peas so they don't fall apart in the dish when it's cooking. Start a small stockpot of water to boiling. Once the water is riotous, drop in your sugar snap peas. Set a kitchen timer for two minutes and prepare an ice bath in a large bowl while it's ticking. When the two minutes are up, use a slotted spoon to immediately transfer the peas to the ice bath. Give them a quick swirl and another minute in the chilly water, then drain and add to the squash and pork. Toss gently to combine, being careful not to smash the tender peas or break up the squash pieces, then turn pour the mixture into a small cassoulet, medium-sized gratin dish, or 9x13 baking pan (glass is preferable).

5. To make the tarragon cream sauce, melt the butter in a medium sauce pan and sauté the minced shallot until they're translucent. Add the wine (I like a barely sweet Chardonnay, one not aged in oak for this sauce), salt, pepper, and both tarragons. Bring to a low boil, then lower the flame to medium or a little higher and cook until the liquid is reduced by a third, probably about 20 minutes, before whisking in the cream. Lower the heat, stirring occasionally for the next five or 10 minutes, until the sauce thickens a little. Pour the sauce over the mix in the casserole dish, gently tossing to distribute evenly.

6. Place the dish in a preheated 350-degree oven. Since everything's already cooked, you shouldn't need more than 30 to 45 minutes to heat through, and it's okay if the top of the dish starts to brown a little. Serve hot in a bowl so that the lovely, aromatic sauce can be swiped up with a light and fluffy biscuit or warm croissant.

Roasted Poblanos with Pulled Pork and Cilantro Lime Cream Sauce

I have always loved Tex-Mex and Mexican food. The former isn't hard to find, the latter—true Mexican food—can be.

I spent some of my early teens living in central California, where my family and I found a love for all things wrapped in tortillas and ladled with salsa. None of it was really Mexican, and it sure as heck wasn't Tex-Mex, but those meals offered insight to both. Moving to the Washington, D.C., metro area in high school allowed for better Mexican food, but I didn't really discover the real deal until a deer hunt took me deep into Mexico. There, on 20,000-acre ranch, one of four like-wise-sized parcels owned by a brother and his sisters and located near nothing but a copper mine far in the distance, the hacienda's diminutive cook provided some of the most unadorned and yet mind-boggling delicious meals for a week. I was so addicted to her refried beans, I made them for three months straight when I got home, trying to get close to the perfection she spooned carefully onto our breakfast and dinner plates.

That trip was many years ago, and I've forgotten the particulars of those fabulous meals beyond the memory of their satisfaction. What I haven't forgotten is how outrageously simple those meals were. No unpronounceable list of ingredients, nothing from a cellophane package or jar, and I don't believe any meal had more than a half-dozen ingredients, including the spices she used. Today, as much as I like a taco or burrito loaded up and sauced, I find that my greater joy in Mexican food lies with those lacking a laundry list of ingredients.

Here's what you'll need, enough to serve four people two poblano halves:

FOR THE POBLANOS

8 full-bodied poblano peppers
2 cups of warm rice
2 cups of pulled pork
2 cups of black beans (drained if from a can)
2 tablespoons of cumin
Salt and pepper to taste

FOR THE CILANTRO LIME CREAM SAUCE

1¼ cup of sour cream
Juice from three limes
1 small jalapeño
1 large bunch of fresh cilantro, including stems

INSTRUCTIONS

1. Take each poblano and slice them at the stem end just enough to remove the seed head as intact as possible. With those removed, you can then slice the peppers in half from the top down, setting the edge of your knife across the diameter of the pepper top, opening and slicing cleanly down along the length of the pepper. Finally, take a paring knife and trim the veiny bit from the inside of each half. Shake or rinse out any loose seeds (dry the peppers with a paper towel if you rinse them), and set the halves in a low-sided casserole or gratin dish.

2. The stuffing for these peppers is easy-peasy. Combine the rice (it's easier to do when the rice is warm), the pulled pork (rough chop this to ½-inch chunks), the beans, cumin, salt and pepper. Divide the mix evenly to fill the pepper halves, then slide your dish into a preheated 350-degree oven for 40 to 45 minutes. The top of the stuffing should be a little crispy and a little brown, and the skin on the peppers should have puckered and wrinkled when they're done.

3. Let the peppers rest while you whip up the sauce in a small food processor or a blender. Add the sour cream, juice from the limes, de-stemmed and de-seeded jalapeño, and chopped cilantro. A couple quick pulses and voila—a gorgeously colored, vibrant sauce.

4. For service, ladle a few tablespoons of the sauce over the hot stuffed poblanos and get everybody a fork and knife. Add in a cold *cervesas* and you might just think you've taken a trip to Mexico for the evening.

Smoked Pozole and Pozole Pie

I'll say up front that pozole (or posole) has been a problem child for me. I first tried this traditional Mexican soup when I lived in San Antonio. I loved it, but life got in the way and I didn't get around to making it myself for the longest time. Then one day I acquired a cookbook on slow cooker recipes that included a recipe for pozole and off to the kitchen I went.

It was a disaster. Not an even-the-dog-won't-eat-it-disaster; it was edible, but it was so bland that I couldn't imagine eating more than the couple spoonfuls I sampled. I talked to friends native to Texas, added this, added that—nothing fixed it.

I made it again, thinking maybe I'd left out some sort of crucial ingredient. Same result. And again with the third batch. I figured I either needed to marry into the family who owned the restaurant where I'd first enjoyed the dish, or declare defeat. And then I wondered if smoking the pork would make a difference.

It did. I have to tell you, this was the very, *very* long way of getting the dog trained, but the results were worth it. That's a heads up: this is probably a two-day recipe for most, or at least one really long day of cooking. Smoking (or slow roasting) just isn't a quick way to do things, especially when there's a large chunk of meat involved. But when you want to make something special, something you can take great pride in after some dedicated stove time, this is a recipe that will win you accolades.

Here's what you'll need:

INGREDIENTS

1 4-pound boneless Boston butt plus
    rub (below)
2 tablespoons of crushed or minced garlic
2 tablespoons of butter
1 medium sweet onion, chopped
1 tablespoon of Mexican oregano
1 tablespoon of ground ancho chili powder
1 ½ tablespoons kosher salt
1 tablespoon smoked paprika
1 tablespoon crushed red chili flakes
1 tablespoon cumin
1 tablespoon onion powder
1 tablespoon garlic powder
1 small cinnamon stick
5 cups of chicken stock
1 32-ounce can of hominy
Optional: Replace chicken stock with pork stock
    using the recipe below

RUB FOR BOSTON BUTT

1 ½ tablespoons kosher salt
1 tablespoon smoked paprika
1 tablespoon crushed red chili flakes
1½ tablespoons cumin
1 tablespoon onion powder
1 tablespoon garlic powder
3 tablespoons cherry pepper chili relish
¾ teaspoon cinnamon

PREPARING YOUR PORK

The pork is the part that takes the most work here. The first thing to do is assemble the rub. Simply combine the ingredients on the list and rub the mixture over every square inch of the butt's surface. You can do this 24 hours ahead of time and refrigerate if you like, but it's also fine to do this the same day.

You no doubt saw the word "smoked" in the recipe title. Yes, you're going to need to smoke the Boston butt, and this will take some time. Like I said, this isn't a soup you assemble in an hour or so. Don't have a smoker? There are a couple options:

- Apparently, you can smoke meat in your oven (though I haven't tried it myself).

  1. Soak a big handful of wood chips (hickory, mesquite, apple, etc.) covered in water for a couple hours and drain all but a little bit of the water.

  2. Spread the wet wood chips in the bottom of a large roasting pan and position a rack above them.

  3. Set your meat on the rack and cover it all the way down the edges of the pan with heavy duty aluminum foil and seal the foil around the pan edges very tightly. Add extra foil as needed to ensure that everything that's going to go underneath the foil stays underneath the foil.

  4. Preheat your oven to 250 degrees and slide in the pan. You'll probably go for at least eight hours (a probe thermometer should give an internal meat reading 170 to 180 degrees). FYI—the smoking will happen during the first 60 to 90 minutes, as the heat dries out the wood chips in the bottom of the roasting pan and they produce smoke, so there's no worries about taking off the aluminum foil after the first couple hours or so and filling your oven and kitchen with smoke. Obviously, taking the meat's temperature at the six-hour mark won't be a problem.

- Smoke on your stovetop. I actually do this with some frequency during the winter months when I don't want to dither with my outside smoker. There are a variety of devices to accomplish this, but most are the flat, rectangular box size good for chicken breasts, fish, or chops. I use a larger domed setup from Nordic Ware that holds a good size hunk of meat—a full chicken or a smaller-sized Boston butt such as the one in this recipe. It works quite well and doesn't cost a lot.

- If you're too timid to do the wood chips/tented foil trick, you can simply fix a *mire poix* of carrots, onions and celery, layer the bottom of a roasting pan with it, place your rubbed Boston butt on top, tightly cover with aluminum foil and slow roast at 250 for six to nine hours. You'll be missing the smoke element, but the slow roasting does all sorts of good things to a Boston butt you're just not going to get with a fast roast.

If you have a smoker outside the house like I do, give your four-pound Boston butt a rub and set in a smoker at 225 degrees. Douse them with smoke a couple times during the first two to three hours. I double wrap it in heavy duty foil at the four-hour mark, then leave it in the smoker for another five hours. You should end up with a beautiful pile of pulled pork.

1. Pork done, you can get to work with the rest of the pozole. Sweat the garlic in the butter in a large stockpot. I did this over a low burner, very slowly taking the garlic from raw to a toasty brown. Once the garlic arrived at that state, I added the chopped onion, sautéing until it was translucent.

2. Add your dried herbs and spices, give it a quick stir and a minute or so on the heat, then add your chicken stock (or pork stock from the optional recipe). Simmer for a while on a medium-low burner, maybe an hour or more.

3. Meanwhile, shred your finished Boston butt, then give the long hunks a rough chop. Note that you don't want to make this chopped pork. Part of the beauty of this soup is the pulled pork bite, so you don't want to undo that too much with your knife.

4. Once the pozole's base has simmered for a while, add your pork. Raise the soup gradually to a gentle bubble, but no need to go to a rolling boil, which could further breakdown your pork and make it mushy. Finally, drain your can of hominy and add this corn goodness to the pozole.

5. Serve this soup piping hot. Traditional garnishes include finely shredded cabbage (I like Savoy), thin-sliced radishes, and wedges of avocado. You can also use sliced green onions and red onion, fresh cilantro (though I prefer to add the cilantro to the soup during the last 15 minutes of cooking, rather than as a garnish on top), or a slice of lime squeezed over the top. I suggest using all of them in various combinations, and setting out bowls of these for your guests to choose from makes for a pretty table. A little cornbread on the side goes well with this light soup, and a chilled picture of salty, lime-tart Margaritas is the perfect beverage accompaniment.

PORK STOCK (OPTIONAL)

It almost seems wrong to use chicken stock with a dish where roasted or smoked pork is so prevalent. While chicken stock works perfectly fine for pork dishes, I made a pork stock for one version of this pozole recipe and it added a definite, concentrated richness to the dish that surpassed the other recipes that used chicken stock. The best thing about this recipe is that you can make it at the same time you're roasting or smoking your Boston butt.

2 cups of diced carrots
1 cup of chopped celery, hearts and leaves included
1 large chopped onion
4 to 6 pork marrow bones
1 cup of red wine (Pinot Noir works well)
1 tablespoon Mexican oregano
1 tablespoon of thyme
3 bay leaves
1 tablespoon of salt
1 tablespoon of black ground pepper

1. Using ingredients from the list above, mix the herbs with your chopped vegetables and spread the mix evenly across the bottom of a roasting pan. Place your marrow bones (you'll likely need a butcher for these) over the veggies (the *mire poix*) and roast for 30 to 45 minutes in an oven set to 400 degrees and remove. The bones should be brown, but the vegetables should not be burned.

2. Move the contents of the roasting pan to a large stockpot and cover with water, bringing the pot to a very low simmer. Lid the pot and leave at this simmer for five to six hours. Do *not* allow the pot to boil. I issue this advice sternly, but I have to give credit to Julia Child for this. Apparently, when making stocks, allowing the pot to boil will result in a muddy-looking finished product. Stock, of course, should be clear.

3. At the end of your long simmer, turn the burner off and allow the stock to cool. Set another stock pot in your sink and place a large, fine mesh sieve over the top of it. Carefully pour the contents of your stock pot into the sieve, which will catch all the solids and leave you with clean stock. Place this stockpot in the refrigerator overnight and you should have a pot full of clear jellied stock in the morning. Use it immediately for the pozole base in place of the chicken stock or spoon it into freezer bags and freeze for future use.

POZOLE PIE

This is a way to liven up leftovers. You can go two ways with this, either a cornbread batter top and bottom or spiced and cheesy polenta or grits.

For the cornbread version, work with a recipe that produces a sweet and moister cake version, rather than a really crumbly one, and make one and a half times the recipe. To wit:

CORNBREAD TOP AND BOTTOM POZOLE PIE

1 cup of fine yellow cornmeal
⅔ cup of sugar (brown sugar works, too)
1 cup of all-purpose flour
1 teaspoon of baking powder
¾ cup of melted butter
1 cup of whole milk or half-and-half
2 cans of creamed corn
1 teaspoon of salt
4 eggs

1. Whisk together all dry ingredients except salt. Add melted butter, half the milk or half-and-half, and creamed corn, stirring to combine. Sprinkle in salt.

2. Whisk in eggs one at a time, then any additional milk necessary to make a thick batter.

3. Pour half the batter into a 9x13 deep-dish casserole, top with enough pozole to come halfway up the side of the dish, then top with the remaining cornbread batter.

4. Bake at 350 for about an hour, up to 90 minutes, until the top crust is golden brown.

CHEESY POLENTA TOP AND BOTTOM POZOLE PIE

4 cups of chicken stock
1 stick of butter
2 cups of yellow polenta or grits (not the instant kind)
2 cups of whole milk
1½ cups of shredded parmesan
2 teaspoons of salt
1 tablespoon of ground black pepper

1. Bring the stock and butter to a boil and add polenta. Stirring constantly, cook until the polenta begins to thicken over medium heat.

2. Gradually add milk, about a half-cup at the time, waiting for the mixture to thicken a bit again before adding more. Before it really stiffens up at the end of your milk supply, whisk in cheese, salt, and pepper, and immediately transfer half of the hot mixture to your 9x13 deep-sided casserole dish.

3. Add enough pozole to come halfway up the sides of the casserole, then top with the remaining hot polenta, spreading it evenly across the top.

4. Bake in a 350-degree oven for about 45 minutes. Top should be light golden brown. If your top is browning too much, cover with foil and continue to bake until the pozole in the middle is piping hot.

PORK SAUSAGE AND GROUND PORK

Apple Scrapple Cinnamon Bread Pudding

If you're not from the East Coast, you're likely unfamiliar with scrapple. That's too bad, for it's yet another terrific use of the whole hog.

As you might infer from the name, scrapple consists of, well, pig scraps. These are the leftover trimmings and such from other prettier cuts that have been mashed together and mixed with cornmeal, fat, and spices, then formed into a terrine or loaf-shaped mold. It's commonly served at breakfast, sliced and fried golden brown on each side. It's terrific with a hot buttered English muffin and a lovely, runny-yolked over easy egg. It's also mmm-*mmmm* good in this dish I whipped up. Here's what you'll need:

INGREDIENTS

2 loaves of Pepperidge Farm Cinnamon Swirl Bread*

2 pounds of scrapple (Jones brand in the green bordered wrapper is the most common one you'll find in your grocer's freezer case)

2 tablespoons of bacon fat

5 medium-sized apples (preferably on the sweet, rather than tart size), peeled, cored and cut into 1 ½-inch chunks

8 large eggs

1 cup of whole milk

1 cup of maple syrup

> *TIP Most bread pudding recipes tell you to use stale bread that you've left out in the open, out of its wrapper, overnight. Most recipes also tell you to refrigerate the dish overnight and bake it in the morning. I find this process to be an enormous waste of time, and I also don't think bread puddings made like this benefit from that night in the fridge; they never seem to cook through correctly for me, and I find them overly soggy in texture.

1. Instead of going the stale bread-overnight soak route, toast your cinnamon swirl bread. Lay the slices of the two loaves across two cookie sheets and set them in a pre-heated 325-degree oven for 20–25 minutes. All I want is to get their inherent moisture out and have the slices take on a nice golden brown color. Set the toasted slices aside to cool.

2. Get your scrapple cooked. Heat a large, nonstick saucier or sauté pan and fry up your scrapple. Two things are important to know here:

   One, the nonstick pan is crucial. Scrapple has very little fat and will stick to a stainless pan like a melted lollipop on a hot dashboard. You can use a little bacon grease if you want or all-natural nonstick spray, but you're best off with a nonstick pan.

   The second thing to know is that while scrapple will brown on the sides that are up against the hot pan surface, the rest will remain a gray color. Also, scrapple doesn't hold together like sausage patties do when they cook. You can carefully flip small slices over to produce two brown sides, but the inside will still be gray—nobody said good tasting food had to be good looking. So flip, brown, stir, whatever. In the end it doesn't really matter. If it's hot through and you've crisped some of it, it's done.

3. For this dish, we really don't care about neat slices. Stir it, browning as much as you can. Once you've gotten crispy brown colors, add your apple chunks. Stir to distribute, leave it to sit on a medium-high burner, stirring again to shift the apples to the bottom of the pan, then lid the pan. You want the apples to get hot through and soften, but don't turn them into mush.

4. While the apples and scrapple are in their last stages of cooking (five minutes with the lid on the pan), whisk together the eggs, milk, and maple syrup.

5. In a deep casserole, take several pieces of the cinnamon toast and break them apart to line the bottom. Spoon on half your apple-scrapple mix and cover with another layer of toasted cinnamon bread. Repeat with the second half of the scrapple mix and top with the last of the toasted cinnamon bread.

6. Gently pour the egg mixture over the top of the assembled pudding. As you pour, insert a table knife gently down to the bottom of the casserole, pushing aside the layers and pouring the egg mix down next to the knife. In this way, you make sure the liquid will get around all the ingredients, rather than puddling in pockets here and there. End by pouring the last bit of liquid over the very top layer of toast.

7. Into a 350-degree preheated oven, lid your casserole for 40 minutes. Take the lid off and bake another 20 minutes until gorgeously brown on top and the pudding has puffed up. There should be no liquid left and the sides of the bread pudding should be pulling away slightly from the sides of the casserole.

8. Let the pudding sit for 10 minutes out of the oven and serve. This makes a super-tasty breakfast or lunch on its own—no need for a sauce as with other bread puddings. This needs nothing more than a cup of excellent coffee to wash it down. It's also a great side dish to pork chops or loin roast slices, producing a savory and welcome change from the ho-hum apple-sauce or sautéed apple accompaniments those main courses usually have.

Chili Gone Green

I was thinking of a way to get out of the red chili rut and come up with something in the white chili range. But the more I thought about it, the more I realized that all the so-called "white" chilis were actually pretty green in their base color. That got the wheels turning, so I hit the grocery store, loaded up my cart, and headed home to make this interesting and still very chili-tasting chili. Here's what you'll need:

INGREDIENTS

5-7 medium zucchini
3 large green bell peppers
4 large poblano peppers
2 jalapeño peppers
2 tablespoons of crushed garlic
1 large sweet onion
1 bunch of green onions, chopped, both whites and greens
2 4-ounce cans of diced green chilies
4 cups of chicken stock

1 package of Frontier Soups White Bean Chili Mix
2 cups of Navy beans
1 ½ pounds of 80/20 ground pork
¼-cup of all-purpose flour
2 tablespoons of cumin
2 tablespoons of garlic powder
2 tablespoons of onion powder
1 cup of smooth peanut butter

INSTRUCTIONS

This requires simple assembly if you do this in a slow cooker like I did. I use a large, seven-quart All-Clad slow cooker, which holds a voluminous amount of food.

1. In the slow cooker, I put in all the vegetables I'd rough chopped—there's no need to go fork- or spoon-sized and I'll get to why in a minute. Then, I added chicken stock and the contents of the Frontier Soups White Bean Chili Mix, beans*, and the other spices. Set slow cooker on a low setting and cook.

2. I started this pot about mid-morning and let it alone for seven hours until 5 p.m. The vegetables should be soft and cooked (though still retaining a bit of color). If the beans still need work, and they did in my case, turn the slow cooker to high and let it go for three more hours.**

3. By this time, it was too late to finish working on this for dinner the same day. Instead, I put a bag of Navy beans in a stock pot and covered them with water before leaving them on a cold stove to soak overnight. I left the slow cooker with its chili on its warm setting (refrigerate overnight if your slow cooker doesn't have this option).

4. The next day, I turned the slow cooker back to a low setting and let it come up in temperature for an hour. The vegetables should be stewed down enough that you can use a stick blender to puree the pot into a beautiful green chili base. Don't have a stick blender? You'll need a second pot, a ladle, and a regular blender to puree your base. Work it in batches, scooping a couple cups of soup out of your slow cooker and adding them to the blender—just remember that if you're working with hot ingredients to take out the little thingamajig in center of your blender lid, or you'll end up with hot chili base everywhere. Transfer each batch of puree to a clean pot until you finish working through all of the base, then put the puree back in your cooking pot or slow cooker. You can also blend it cold if you had refrigerated your base overnight.

5. With my slow cooker still set at low, I prepared my ground pork. I heated bacon fat in a large saucier and added the ground pork to brown. As it neared completion, I poured off most of the fat, added flour and spices, whisking to make a roux of sorts. I then added this to the puree in the slow cooker, along with my nicely soaked Navy beans (the beans in the batch that had been pureed along with the vegetables and stock adds body and thickness to the chili). Change the setting to high, stirring in the cup of peanut butter during the last hour (see my explanation for peanut butter in the recipe "Roasted Pork Tenderloin Chili," page 74).

6. Two hours later, I had a silky, nicely flavored, and mild chili with the tender bite of pork and soft Navy beans—a totally refreshing change from the spicy red fare I usually make. I ate this with a sweet cornbread muffin I crumbled in the bottom of a bowl filled with hot wild rice. I also ate it with a batch of homemade nachos I made with refried beans and Monterey Jack cheese instead of salsa or *pico de gallo*. Fabulous each and every way and a pretty damn healthy chili on top of that.

*TIP I don't use a lot of pre-packaged foods, but chili tends to be an exception. While I certainly create the majority of my chilies from scratch, I also usually use chili "kits." They almost always have the right spice base combination, and though I'll add to it, the mix in the kits helps to build the correct flavor foundation. You don't have to use the brand I have listed here; any white bean chili packaged mix will do.

**TIP The beans not being done were completely my fault—I often forget to soak dry beans overnight. If you make chili on a stove rather than in a slow cooker, however, this is usually not a problem since the heat will be higher and you'll be bringing your dish to a boil for a while. Alternatively you can also use canned beans.

Chorizo and Shellfish Chowder

I've never been a fan of Manhattan clam chowder. In general I prefer thick stews and soups, so given a choice, I'll pick New England clam chowder over Manhattan every time. At the same time, I have to be honest and say my first exposure to the Manhattan variety was probably nothing more than the can of Campbell's my mother accidentally purchased from time to time when I was a kid, and I was always disappointed in the few tiny bits of clam those cans seemed to have. But in early winter I found myself working on this book and thought I ought to give the Manhattan a whirl . . . but how to work pork into it? The answer: chorizo.

Here's what you'll need:

INGREDIENTS

2 pints of cherry tomatoes
3 tablespoons of butter
3 tablespoons of chopped garlic
2 cups of fresh chopped clams
1 cup of fresh shucked oysters
1 ½ cups of fresh or pre-cooked
    shucked mussels
1 ½ cups of fresh medium-sized scallops
2 to 3 cups of clam stock

1 tablespoon of thyme
1 tablespoon of garlic powder
1 tablespoon of onion powder
1 teaspoon of ground cayenne pepper
Salt and pepper to taste
1 ½ pounds of soft chorizo
1 32-ounce can of whole peeled tomatoes
¼ cup tomato paste
3 cups of chicken stock

INSTRUCTIONS

1. Pour the sweetest cherry tomatoes you can find into a gratin or low-sided casserole dish in a single layer. Drizzle with a bit of olive oil, sprinkle with sea salt, and set in a pre-heated 350-degree oven. Roast for about 45 minutes until the tomatoes have split and their juices are rendering around them.

2. While the tomatoes are roasting, start your stockpot. Melt three tablespoons of butter over medium low heat and add chopped garlic. Sauté the garlic low and slow until it turns a light to medium golden brown, stirring frequently to keep it from burning.

3. As soon as the garlic arrives at the desired color and aroma, add your clams, juice and all. You can get clams from the grocer that are already shucked and minced (this is in fact a nice chop, with generous hunks of clam), coming in their natural juices. I'm fortunate to live on the East Coast now and have a regular year-round supply of fresh seafood and shellfish. But having also spent my time living in various Midwest states, I know such convenience is a luxury that someone living in Kansas or Wisconsin simply doesn't have. There are a few solutions to this:

- Though fresh is always the option, there are good canned clams out there, as well as frozen. Do your research and buy accordingly.

- Scallops, mussels, and oysters are all frozen. Look for wild caught and flash frozen shellfish, and, as with canned clams, do research into what brands are high quality. Do *not* use the smoked oysters that come in a tin. While these gems are good for snacking, the smoking process totally changes the texture of the oyster and they will not complement this dish.

- Online ordering. This won't be cheap, in part because seafood is generally expensive, but also because the packaging and overnight shipping is costly. But if you insist on freshness, there are dozens of fishmongers on either coast who will ship you any fish or shellfish you need.

- Note: Poor quality shellfish will either have no taste at all or be too pungent, and it can also be tough or rubbery. So if you can't buy fresh, shop carefully and sample in small batches. Seafood isn't like a poor cut of beef you can just cook longer or slower and then sauce the daylights out of it. Bad seafood is just that—bad.

4. Now you've got your clams in the pot with all that warm, buttery garlic. Raise the temperature and let the clams simmer gently for 20 to 30 minutes, giving them a chance to marry well with the garlic. Add in the rest of your shellfish (thawed, if you started with frozen product), including their juices, a can of good clam stock (I used Bar Harbor brand), and the herbs and spices. Maintain the slow simmer for 45 minutes to an hour.

5. Meanwhile, sauté your chorizo in a separate pan. I buy my chorizo in links, slit the casings lengthwise, and turn the loose meat out into the pan. If you have access to a good quality firmer chorizo and prefer to use that, neatly slice those chorizo links into fork-sized bites and sauté until cooked through.

6. When the chorizo is done, add it and its renderings (unless you have a really fatty chorizo, in which case use a slotted spoon to keep too much grease from spoiling the chowder) to the simmering seafood, followed by your roasted cherry tomatoes and their juices, the can of whole peeled tomatoes and its juices, the tomato paste, and enough chicken stock and clam juice to cover the ingredients and provide extra body.

7. Raise the temperature to medium high and gradually bring the chowder to a happy boil, stirring occasionally. The cherry tomatoes will break down further and you can take your stirring spoon and cut the bigger peeled tomatoes from the can in half after they cook through during the boil. Reduce the heat and simmer on low for at least an hour before serving.*

8. For service, a steaming bowl of this gorgeous, decadent chowder by itself is fine, though you could add tasty crackers if you want a little crunch and grain or use bread to sop up the leftover broth. I had some sweet corn muffins on hand when I made this, and I crumbled one in the bottom of the bowl before ladling in the soup, and it was just *wonderful*. A little rice and some good fettuccini noodles are also good accompaniments.

*TIP I did what I do with most of my soups, creating this throughout an afternoon, simmering for several hours in the early evening, and then turning the burner off and letting the pot sit overnight on the cold stove. I refrigerated the pot in the morning, then reheated for dinner the next night. While the Food and Drug Administration might frown on this practice, I've never sickened anyone nor gotten sick myself—even with a pot left on the stove overnight in the summer—and I truly believe flavors in ingredient-rich concoctions like this benefit greatly and better complement each other when the dish is allowed to progress from the gradual build of assembled ingredients to the quick boil, long simmer, cold overnight sit, and morning refrigeration.

Chorizo Soft Breakfast Tacos

Breakfast tacos are a staple in areas of the country where there's a defined Hispanic population. San Antonio comes to mind. I lived there for three years, and there seemed to be a small Jalisco grill on every corner and in every strip mall. Most were pretty good, even if ordering in English was sometimes a challenge.

I frequented a couple of these small family-run enterprises every morning on the way to work and I always ordered the same thing: refried beans, eggs, and potato soft tacos. Doesn't sound like much, does it? It wasn't. I count four ingredients including the soft flour tortilla, five if you drizzle on red or green sauce. But they were delicious, far better than the over-fried fare at big fast-food chains. They were also filling in a way a bowl of oatmeal can never be.

I had food of the same simplicity on a hunting trip deep into the copper mining country of Mexico. We were served simple breakfast tacos by a tiny lady who looked like an ancient Mayan statue brought to life. Another batch was wrapped in foil to be eaten cold for lunch, high in the hills. Sometimes they were just beans and other times there was cold fried fish or leftover steak in them. All were amazingly good, the few flavors standing up on their own with nothing more than salt and pepper to enliven them. One day, in between hunts, I watched our diminutive chef in the kitchen. She spoke not one word of English and spent her days making tortillas and refried beans by hand. Her weathered hands flew from masa to tortilla press and spoon to pot with an effortless flair only a lifetime of routine cooking can wrought; her beans were so good I spent three months working to recreate them at home before I came close to the buttery smoothness hers had.

The point of this is that putting together something like this is so simple and so easy that you'll wonder why you never thought to venture away from the American standard of bacon and eggs before—and you'll likely never order a McAnything ever again.

You can mix this up if you want, but if you really want these breakfast bites to sing, keep it as that Mexican cook and the San Antonio grills do: simple. Resist adding the fajita accoutrements of cheese, peppers, onions, sour cream, and guacamole. Sometimes, less is more. Here's what you'll need to feed four:

5 chorizo links, the soft kind
2 ½ cups of cold, cubed boiled potatoes

1 16-ounce can of refried beans
8 6-inch flour tortillas

INSTRUCTIONS

1. Sauté your chorizo over medium heat. I like to take my chorizo links out of their casings and break the meat up in the pan. For this dish, don't break it down to where it was in its original ground state. Instead, leave it in fork-sized chunks for a more flavorful bite.

2. When the chorizo is nearly done (remember, chorizo won't change color when it cooks except to darken a little, so when it's hot through it's done), pour off the excess fat if your chorizo has a high fat content, but not all of it to preserve the chorizo's spices and flavors in that fat. Add cubed boiled potatoes.

3. Brown the potatoes so they take on some of the color of the chorizo. You can lid the pan, but stir every couple minutes to keep things from sticking, especially if your chorizo hasn't rendered out a lot of fat.

4. Open your can of refried beans and spoon it over the top. Put the lid on the pan for five minutes or so, which will warm the beans to the point they can be easily stirred into the chorizo and potatoes. Next, put the lid back on the pan, stirring occasionally, until all is piping hot, then remove the pan from the flame and let it sit a few minutes to allow the dish to thicken, which will ensure that the mix will stay in the tortillas instead of running out the end and down your hand.

5. Zap your tortillas in the microwave on high for 20 seconds; you could also wrap them in foil and pop them in a toaster oven to warm while you're making the chorizo mix. When you're ready to eat, spoon a good helping of the chorizo mix into the center of each warm tortilla, fold up, and eat. Wrap tightly in foil and take with you for the commute or breakfast at your desk. I promise you won't be going through the drive-through lane of your breakfast express anytime soon with these breakfast tacos.

Chourico, Rice, and Lentil Cassoulet

I once read that even avid cooks have 10 to 15 recipes they turn to and make time and time again, rotating them in and out of weeknight meals and weekend fare on a regular basis. These are the recipes you can make without a book or papered list of ingredients—you know these dishes on an intimate level wrought from years of repetition, both in their preparation and their results on the plate.

One of my rinse-and-repeat dishes is 15-bean soup and kielbasa. It's not hard: You buy the bag of beans that says "15-Bean-Soup-Mix" on the packaging, add chicken stock, kielbasa, the flavoring packet that comes with the beans or some garlic and onion powder, a can of chopped tomatoes, and shredded cabbage, and voila—along with a plate of hot rice, dinner is served.

Chourico, for those who haven't come across it, is a sausage of Portuguese origin. I find mine in packs of two large links, much like kielbasa, but with the ends of the casings twisted and intact instead of being sliced off. Its firmness is very similar to kielbasa—like a firm artisanal hotdog with a bit of snap to the casing as you bite through a cooked piece—but this is a heavily spiced sausage that wears the bright orange-red color of a heavily spiced chorizo. The flavor profile is also like chorizo, though not identical. I like it because I get a sausage with a great depth of flavor and also with a texture that works well in a dish like this. This cassoulet recipe also features a rice and lentil mix. I used a mix called "Old World Pilaf" made by a company called Lundborg, with an ingredient list that incuded whole grain brown rice, whole grain Wehani rice, whole grain black Japonica rice, lentils, black-eyed peas, and green and yellow split peas. Here's what you'll need:

INGREDIENTS

1 pound of chourico sausage
1 large sweet onion
1 16-ounce bag or box of mixed rice and lentils

1 cup of hot mustard
1 24-ounce box of chicken stock/broth
Water as needed

1. Slice chourico links in half along their lengths. Next, chop those links into ¼-inch wide slices—they'll look like half moons, which are easier to handle on the fork or spoon and in the mouth. Put the chopped chourico in a small- to medium-sized covered casserole dish. Rough chop your onion and add to the dish, along with the rice, bean, and lentil mix.

2. Add the cup of hot mustard and chicken stock. Stir to combine and evenly distribute. There should be enough liquid to cover the solid ingredients by a half-inch—you've got to have enough for the rice to cook through—so add some water or broth as needed. Lid your cassoulet and slide the dish into a 375-degree oven.

3. Once in the oven, stir the cassoulet at the 45-minute mark (there should still be plenty of liquid), and go another 30 minutes (with the dish lidded). Check again for a taste test and to see if the rice is cooked through. If a tad undercooked, add more water as needed to the cassoulet, lid, and set it in the oven for another 30 minutes.*

4. For service, spoon an ample helping into a bowl, maybe top with chopped green onions for a crisp bite, and pour a cold beer into a tall glass. Dinner, my friends, is served.

*TIP You can also cook your cassoulet on the stove top, bringing the dish to a boil unlidded and stirring frequently, then lidding the pot and reducing the flame, stirring frequently until all the liquid is absorbed and the rice is al dente. Another option is to dump all your ingredients in a slow cooker, set it, and forget it on high for four to five hours or six to seven hours on low.

Hot Italian Sausage and Tapenade Appetizers

I have a penchant for overcooking. I'll buy four or eight of something or look at the ingredients for a recipe and think, *Well, that's never going to be enough*. I even look at the giant pots the chefs use on *Diners, Drive-Ins and Dives* and think I need to add those to the arsenal of kitchen gear I have. That is utterly absurd, since I live by myself.

One of my solutions to this gluttony of ingredients is to work with a smaller stockpot. My go-to is usually the largest cast iron behemoth Le Creuset makes, so I "forced" myself to buy a two-quart stockpot from Williams-Sonoma's own line of stainless cookware. That solved the quantity problem on the *finished* end, but it hasn't curbed my penchant for doubling the ingredients on any given dish.

And so it was with a recent batch of spicy spaghetti I recently made. The pot full, I still had a couple cups of cooked, ground, hot Italian sausage in the pan. I dug through the pantry and came up with this:

INGREDIENTS

1 cup of ground hot Italian sausage (a spicier sausage pairs well with the tapenade)
1 cup of mixed olive tapenade

1 soft French baguette
1 container of soft mozzarella discs*
1 cup of cherry tomatoes

> *TIP When choosing mozzarella, use the really soft kind that comes packed in water, rather than the kind that has the texture of string cheese or that you would shred for pizza. Why? The super-soft type melts *into* the sausage mix, rather than just melting on top, which means that when you bit into it, the cheese doesn't come sliding off when you take a bite.

INSTRUCTIONS

The quantities are a little strange for this. You need neither the entire baguette nor the full containers of cherry tomatoes and mozzarella, unless you're serving this to a crowd, in which case knock yourself out. For just you and a special someone, six little rounds make a nice start before a meal.

1. Pulse the cooked sausage in a food processor to break up the bigger chunks and even out the grind. I also added a little of the cold fat from the cooking process (you can use cold bacon fat), to help bind the sausage with the olive mix and let it moisten the bread as the appetizers cooked. In a bowl, combine your cooked hot Italian sausage with the tapenade (I used jar tapenade).

2. Slice your baguette into ⅓-inch thick discs. The baguette should be a softer kind, which will provide a nice chew without you having to fight the bread like a hyena tearing off a chunk of hindquarter from a freshly killed impala. Allow two to three pieces per guest.

3. With a teaspoon, heap a helping of sausage and tapenade over each bread slice. Top with a section of cheese and pop in a preheated 325-degree oven for 10 to 15 minutes until the sausage mix is hot, the cheese melted, and the baguette slices golden on the bottom. I helped the toasting along by positioning my slices on a wire rack over a drip pan, which allowed hot air to get at the bottom.

4. When the slices are cool enough to handle but still warm, place half a cherry tomato on the slice and nosh away.

Pesto Pork and Chicken Meatloaf with Vodka Sauce

I've made meatloaf with dozens of different ingredients. I remember the first night I had enough stuff unpacked in my new house in Texas to get a dinner cooked, I whipped up a meatloaf that included a can of mushroom soup and an eight-ounce container of pico de gallo— and it *rocked*.

That may sound like a weird way to make meatloaf, but the word really says it all: You need meat in the form of a loaf. I think how you get to the loaf part is totally up for interpretation. Here's one of my interpretations, one that works well when the weather's warmer and you're looking for a meal that won't weigh you down. I've done this recipe using all pork and it has always turned out perfectly fine, but this version with ground chicken is a little lighter and works better for a weeknight dinner during the late spring and summer when you're tired of eating cold salads.

INGREDIENTS

¾ pound of 80/20 ground pork
¾ pound of ground chicken
8 ounces of pesto
1 tablespoon of garlic powder
1 tablespoon of onion powder
2 teaspoons of salt
1 tablespoon of ground black pepper

3 large eggs
2 cups of garlic and herb bread crumbs
1 32-ounce jar of vodka sauce
Optional: 1 cup of fresh basil leaves, 1 cup of minced pine nuts, one cup of grated parmesan, combined

1. In a large mixing bowl, combine the two meats thoroughly. Do this with the meat cold from the refrigerator so that the heat from your hands doesn't turn the mixture to mush. Add the pesto and spices, crack in your eggs, and toss in your breadcrumbs. Mix it together by hand, kneading and squeezing until combined. Two or three minutes is all it should take; don't overwork it.

2. Place the mixture in a full size bread-loaf pan and smooth the top with your fingers or a rubber spatula. If you are one if those who just can't make a meatloaf without dressing it with some sort of sauce before you put it in the oven, then top the loaf with the optional combination of fresh basil, crushed pine nuts, and parmesan, pressing the topping down into the top of the loaf. Do *not* dress with additional pesto as the olive oil in the pesto will cause you to end up with an oily, soggy, gross mess.

3. Preheat your oven to 350 degrees, slide in your loaf pan (set it on a jellyroll pan if the loaf pan is really full, to prevent any rendered fat from boiling over onto your burner elements. One hour and the top of the loaf should be prettily browned and the rendered fat in the pan bubbling. Heat up your vodka sauce during the last five minutes while the meatloaf is cooking.

4. Remove the loaf pan from the oven and drain and dispose of the rendered fat. Let the loaf sit in the pan for five minutes, before inverting it onto a serving dish. Slice it and serve. I served mine over a bed of tender Romaine hearts, then ladled the hot vodka sauce over the top, which adds a richness that is not as heavy as a cream sauce. It makes for a great meal on a really warm August evening, and the leftover cold loaf will also make terrific sandwiches the next day.

Pork and Ricotta Meatballs

There are few staples in American table fare that unquestionably fall into the category of comfort food. Fresh-baked bread with butter, macaroni and cheese, sausage gravy and biscuits . . . and meatballs.

There are as many ways to make meatballs as there are to make burgers and I admit that I probably never make them the same way twice. That said, this is one iteration I took the trouble to write down as soon as the meatballs came out of the oven, because they were just that good. Here's what you'll need for a very large batch of meatballs (about 40 golf ball-sized meatballs, plus six super large rounds for meatball subs (see the end of this recipe).

INGREDIENTS

1 ½ pounds of 80/20 ground chuck
1 ½ pounds of 80/20 ground pork
1 pound of spicy hot Italian sausage
1 large bunch of fresh basil
1 large bunch of fresh flat-leaf Italian parsley
2 tablespoons of crushed red pepper flakes
2 tablespoons of dried oregano
2 tablespoons of garlic powder

3 tablespoons of onion powder
1 ½ tablespoons of fine sea salt
1 ½ tablespoons of cracked black pepper
4 tablespoons of crushed garlic
2 to 3 cups of fresh ricotta cheese
4 to 5 large eggs
3 to 4 cups of garlic and herb breadcrumbs

INSTRUCTIONS

1. With your hands, mix the three meats in a large mixing bowl, preferably one that's wide at the top so you can reach in easily and turn the mixture as you go. Meats should be refrigerator cold, so take a break from time to time to let your hands warm up. The ground chuck and ground beef should be of equal grind and, thus, easy to mix together. The sausage may take a little work, as you'll probably only find it in link version. Slit the link cases lengthwise and squeeze out the meat to mix in with the other two. Don't overwork the mix.

2. Mince the fresh basil and parsley; I put mine in the food processor and pulse until fine, but you can also give it a consistent chop with a knife. With the mixed meats spread out across the diameter of the bowl to provide as much surface area as possible, sprinkle on all the dried herbs and spices and the crushed garlic.

3. Gently mix the new additions into the meat, folding and squeezing until the herbs are nicely distributed, probably a half-dozen kneadings or so. Again, resist overworking.

4. Now add in the ricotta and eggs. You can scramble the eggs ahead of time, but I add them whole and don't notice a problem with it. Fold and squeeze until you see an even distribution of ground meat, white ricotta, and green herbs. The mixture should be wet, even a little gooey.

5. Work two cups of breadcrumbs into the mixture. Add more as you need until you can form a golf ball-sized meatball that isn't mushy and yet holds together completely on its own without wetness.

6. Line a large jellyroll pan with parchment paper and preheat the oven to 375 degrees. Roll your meatballs and place them on the parchment paper evenly spaced out from one another. When the oven is heated, slide in the tray, being careful not to roll the balls. Check at the 20-minute mark, but you likely won't go any further than 30 minutes. The meatballs should be lightly browned and even glistening. Unless you're going to eat the meatballs immediately, it's okay to leave them just a hair undercooked, which will help keep them tender (see the "Pork Bolognese with Fettuccine" recipe on page 139, and the "Ultimate Meatball Grinder" recipe on page 136.) They should not be greasy and should not fall apart when you bite into them. Instead, they should be succulent, packed with flavor and, if I do say so myself, damn near irresistible.

THE ULTIMATE MEATBALL GRINDER

If you reference the recipe for "Pork and Ricotta Meatballs" (page 133), you'll see I made a large batch of meatballs that I used in the dish "Pork Bolognese with Fettuccine" (page 139). I deliberately made six oversized meatballs just so I could make a meatball grinder. "Grinder" is what they call a long, stuffed sandwich in the part of New England where I live. You may call them a submarine sandwich, a hero, or a hoagie. No matter the name, this is the way to make the best meatball sandwich you've ever had. The ingredient list below is for six large meatballs, enough for two big grinders:

INGREDIENTS

¾ pound of 80/20 ground chuck

¾ pound of 80/20 ground pork

½ pound of spicy hot Italian sausage

¼ cup of finely minced of fresh basil

¼ cup of finely minced fresh flat-leaf
    Italian parsley

½ tablespoon of crushed red pepper flakes

2 teaspoons of dried oregano

1 tablespoons of garlic powder

1 ½ tablespoons of onion powder

2 teaspoons of fine sea salt

2 teaspoons of cracked black pepper

2 tablespoons of crushed garlic

1 ½ cups of fresh ricotta cheese

2 large eggs

1 to 2 ½ cups of spicy breadcrumbs

2 6- to 8-inch soft grinder rolls

2 ½ cups of spicy marinara sauce

8 slices of cooked bacon (preferably not very
    crispy, but cooked through)

8 thick slices of provolone (not smoked)

1 ½ cups of shredded mozzarella

INSTRUCTIONS

1. Using your hands, mix the three meats in a large mixing bowl. Meats should be refrigerator cold, so take a break from time to time to let your hands warm up. The ground chuck and ground beef should be of equal grind and, thus, easy to mix together. The sausage may take a little work to incorporate, as you'll likely only find it in link version, so slit the link cases lengthwise and squeeze out the meat to mix in with the other two. Don't overwork the mix; just go enough so that you don't end up with meatballs that have only one meat and not the others in them.

2. Mince the fresh basil and parsley; I put mine in the food processor and pulse until fine, but you can also give it a consistent chop with a knife. With the mixed meats spread out across the diameter of the bowl to provide as much surface area as possible, sprinkle on all the dried herbs and spices and the crushed garlic.

3. Gently mix the new additions into the meat, folding and squeezing until you the herbs are nicely distributed, probably a half-dozen kneadings or so. Again, resist overworking.

4. Now add in the ricotta and the eggs. I add them whole, but you can whisk ahead of time if you like. Fold and squeeze until you see an even distribution of ground meat, white ricotta, and green herbs. The mixture should be wet, even a little gooey.

5. Mix in the breadcrumbs, starting with one cup and working it in. Add more as you need, but the minute you can form a meatball that isn't mushy and yet holds together completely on its own without wetness or that sticky egg feel, you're done.

6. Line a jellyroll pan or a gratin dish with parchment paper and preheat the oven to 375 degrees. Form your meatballs. Since these are for a grinder, go large, about twice the size of a golf ball, but not as big as a Yankee's baseball. Place the meatballs an equal distance apart on the parchment paper and slide them into the oven, being careful not to roll the balls. Check at the 30-minute mark. The meatballs should be lightly browned and maybe even glistening, but they should be just a hair undercooked, which will keep them tender. They should not be greasy.

7. Let the meatballs cool on the counter to room temperature. While the meatballs are cooling, prep your sandwich. Take your grinder roll and slice it in half lengthwise. Open up the roll and butter the inside of each half, then add a bit of garlic salt. Lightly toast the roll, either in a toaster oven or in the regular oven, until the buttered side is just barely golden brown. Remove and set aside.

8. Warm the marinara sauce in a sauté pan. While the sauce is warming, cut each of the meatballs in half, cleanly, with a sharp knife. If you've formed the meatballs correctly and left them undercooked just a smidge, they should not fall apart when sliced and should be a little pink on the inside.

9. When the sauce is bubbly, lay each of the meatball halves cut side down in the sauce and lid the pan. Leave there for three or four minutes, enough to build up steam and rewarm the meatballs. Lift the lid and spoon some marinara sauce over the top of the meatballs, re-lid the pan, and let simmer another three to five minutes.

10. Split your grinder rolls nearly in half and lay them open. On one side lay three to four slices of bacon. Next, lay two slices of provolone on *each* half of both grinder rolls (four slices of cheese per sandwich, with cheese on each side). With a spatula, lay meatball halves in a row down the length of the grinder roll, down the middle, then spoon a bit of hot marinara sauce over the top (but don't soak the rolls). Sprinkle half the shredded mozzarella over on top of the meatballs and along the sides.

11. On a cookie sheet or jelly roll pan lined with foil or parchment paper, set each sandwich open-faced. Slide the sandwiches under a hot broiler for a few minutes, until the mozzarella is melted and bubbling, and remove. When the halves are cool enough to handle, fold the halves together, spoon a little more marinara sauce down the middle, and grab a stack of napkins.

Pork Bolognese with Fettuccini

Let's face it. Unless it's a ravioli or tortellini, even flavored pasta doesn't really taste like much. As much as we love those glorious noodles, they're not much more than a vehicle for sauces, meats, and other lovely edibles.

I have several authentic and old school Italian cookbooks. I learned how to make a proper Bolognese from one, and it tends to be my go-to sauce when I'm feeling the need for a plain dish of spaghetti. But switching out the beef and veal for pork made it even better. Here's what you'll need.

INGREDIENTS

15 Roma tomatoes

Olive oil

Salt and ground black pepper to taste

2 pounds of 80/20 ground pork

2 cups of finely minced carrots

1 cup of finely minced celery (hearts and their leaves preferred)

2 cups of finely minced onion

¼ cup of all-purpose flour

2 cups of bold red wine (a cabernet is preferable)

2 tablespoons of crushed red pepper flakes

2 tablespoons of dried oregano

4 tablespoons of crushed garlic

2 tablespoons of garlic powder

3 tablespoons of onion powder

1 large bunch of fresh flat-leaf Italian parsley chopped very fine

1 large bunch of fresh basil, chopped very fine

1 cup of milk

½ cup of creamy peanut butter*

8 ounces of good-quality fettuccini noodles

Optional: 2 16-ounce cans of Great Northern white bean and two cups of shredded mozzarella for baking

As I have mentioned on page 74, one of the secrets to great chili is adding a bit of peanut butter. So what does this have to do with my take on Bolognese? A lot. Tomatoes are fickle things. There are dozens of varieties with a wide range of acidity and sweetness levels, but descriptions of the various tomatoes in your grocery store don't tell you much. Even when you have a general idea of what a particular tomato should taste like, that flavor doesn't always come to, ahem, fruition. Basically, it can be a crap shoot when cooking with tomatoes in volume. That's where peanut butter comes in. I'm sure that every long-lineaged Italian reading this is cringing at the thought, but it you are working with a bland bunch of tom's or a variety that is too sour or exhibits a high acidity level, a little peanut butter can rectify those issues. The best thing is that while I can smell the aroma of the melted peanut butter in a hot tomato-based sauce, I can't *taste* it. So, the lesson here is add it if you need it, don't if you don't, but have it on hand because it can save your sauce.

INSTRUCTIONS

1. Roast your Roma tomatoes. Split them in half down their long sides and place them cut side down in a low-sided casserole or gratin dish in a single layer. Drizzle with olive oil and sprinkle with sea salt, then roast in a 350-degree oven for 1 ¼ to 1 ½ hours, until the tomatoes are very wilted and their roasting pans full of juice. Set aside to cool.

2. Brown your pork in the stockpot you'll be making the sauce in. When it's browned, lift out the meat with a slotted spoon and set it aside to drain on a plate lined with paper towels. Keep a half-cup of the rendered pork fat in the stockpot but dispose of the rest.

3. To the hot pork fat in the stock pot, add your finely minced carrots, celery, and onion. (I need to stress that these should be *very* finely minced. A food processor works best for this, as you can get them down almost to a paste. They should disappear in the sauce as it cooks.) This, of course, is a *mire poix*, but with the vegetables more finely chopped than in other dishes. Sauté in the fat until very tender. There should be no residual water from the vegetables sweating, and the mixture should start to lightly brown. Once the vegetables are at this stage, whisk in the quarter-cup of flour to produce a quick roux.

4. As you're cooking down the vegetables, get the tomatoes ready for the sauce. Working in batches, puree the roasted tomatoes and all the juices in a blender until very smooth.

5. When you've completed adding the flour to the vegetables and whisking it into a roux, add in your tomato puree. Stir to combine, then add the wine, browned pork, spices, and the chopped parsley and basil.

6. Slowly bring this mixture to a gentle bubble, keeping a lid on the pot to keep spatter down and stirring from time to time to make sure nothing's sticking to the bottom. Keep that gentle boil for 15 minutes or so, stirring more frequently. This will help the vegetables in the *mire poix* to further reduce and become part of the sauce, rather than pieces in it. Reduce the flame to low, put a lid on the pot, and let it simmer for at least an hour, though longer is preferable. A longer simmer makes for a smoother texture and taste.

7. Up to an hour before serving, add in the milk and peanut butter and increase the heat a bit, stirring from time to time. This doesn't make this a creamed tomato sauce, but a little milk is vital to a good Bolognese sauce.

8. Boil your pasta, either fresh or dried, until *al dente* and drain. Dish up a good amount and smother with this wonderful, aromatic, gorgeous sauce. Add some meatballs from the "Pork and Ricotta Meatballs" recipe on page 133, then break off a hunk of hot buttered garlic bread, pour yourself a glass of really good wine, and call it a day—a *really* good day.**

TIP Want a little extra protein and texture in this dish? Toss in two drained 6-ounce cans of white or cannellini beans and combine with your Bolognese noodles, then pour into a casserole dish and top with the shredded mozzarella. Bake at 350 until bubbly, 30 to 45 minutes.

Porkestrone

Minestrone is one of my favorite soups; it has that "everybody in the pool" thing going on—vegetables, beans, pasta, potatoes. It is without doubt a hearty and filling dish, one with lots going on in the texture department.

Contrary to popular belief, there are more than a few variations on the usual tomato-based version most of us encounter. I've experimented with a couple recipes that lean towards green, as well as a couple different takes on the red, and what I've discovered is that no matter what version and what chunky ingredients there are, they all still have that very distinctive platform that your tongue expects when you think about the word minestrone.

Being Italian in origin, whatever minestrone recipe you choose to work with, they can all benefit from the incorporation of pork. The ingredient list for this one I came up with looks a little long, but the finished product is on the peasant-simple end of the style spectrum. You'll enjoy this on a cold winter evening, with fresh baked focaccia or thick sourdough bread on the side for dipping. Here's what you'll need.

INGREDIENTS

2 tablespoons of extra virgin olive oil
4 ounces of diced pancetta
2 pounds of 80/20 course ground pork
Salt and ground black pepper to taste
1 tablespoon of fresh garlic, crushed or minced
¼ cup all-purpose flour
2 28-ounce cans of whole peeled tomatoes
    with their juices
2 16-ounce cans of cannellini beans
2 6-ounce cans of tomato paste
32 ounces of chicken stock
1 cup of fresh basil, chopped

1 tablespoon of dried oregano
Leaves from several sprigs of fresh oregano
¾ tablespoon of garlic powder
¾ tablespoon of onion powder
2 stalks of celery, plus some celery hearts,
    chopped
1 small bunch Italian flat-leaf parsley, chopped
2 medium red onions, diced
½ a medium head of Savoy cabbage
5 large red chard leaves
Water as needed

1. In a large stockpot, gently heat the extra virgin olive oil. I use a very large Le Creuset stockpot, which I believe should not be warmed dry. Once you've gotten it a bit warm and its viscosity has increased, add the pancetta and ground pork, breaking up the pork with a flat-edged wooden spoon as it cooks. You can also salt and add a few twists of cracked ground pepper.

2. Once the pork has cooked through, drain off most of the excess liquid fat, leaving just a bit, maybe a quarter- to a half-cup, behind. Add crushed or minced garlic, stirring frequently over a medium flame for 15 to 20 minutes to let the garlic soften in texture and mellow in flavor.

3. Sprinkle on your flour and whisk to combine. The liquid fat will quickly disappear and the contents of your pot will look like a paste. What you're accomplishing here is a roux of sorts that serves as a thickening agent. To be honest, not a lot of minestrone recipes use a roux, but I'm not fan of really brothy soups. However, if you prefer a soup like minestrone to really be brothy, skip the flour.

4. Add the rest of the ingredients. When I'm crafting a busy soup like this, I add the bigger components one at a time, letting them meld with the ones before them at a simmer for a half-hour or so before adding the next. You can certainly add these all at once, but if you have the time, add them in the following in order, giving each one a half-hour simmer with a bit of stirring.

   - Both cans of whole peeled tomatoes with their juice
   - The cannellini beans, with its liquid (you can drain if you don't want this diluting the thickness of the soup)
   - Both cans of tomato paste
   - Half the chicken stock
   - All of the herbs, spices, and the chopped celery, parsley, and onion

5. Leave the soup on a low simmer—steaming and very gently bubbling—for a good hour or more to allow everything to come together. I generally start this kind of dish around noon, building throughout the afternoon so that it's ready for dinner.*

6. At this stage, gradually bring the soup up to a rolling boil. Lid the pot to prevent tomato spatter, but you also have to stir frequently. Once there, add in the chopped cabbage and chard leaves and reduce the heat back down to medium low to simmer. Add the remainder of the chicken stock as need be to keep an inch or so of broth above the solid ingredients as the soup settles and reduces. Stir to keep anything from sticking to the bottom, though a lid on the pot will help.

7. For serving, add a hunk of thick bread to mop up the bowl at the end of your second helping. Of course, you can add pasta, as many minestrones do. A very small orzo or ditalini is a common addition, but a way to take this dish out of the mainstream would be to use medium-sized shells. These fit nicely on a soup spoon and will hold a mouthful of the minestrone inside them. If you're used to potatoes in your minestrone, ladle this over hot gnocchi.

---

*TIP   As I've said, you can certainly assemble this more quickly and have dinner ready in an hour, but like most soups of this sort, the flavors will be better the next day. As you'll see in other recipes, I usually finish the assembly of my stews and soups by dinner or early evening, but then turn off the burner and let the pot sit on the stove overnight. I refrigerate it in the morning, then reheat it for dinner the *following* night.

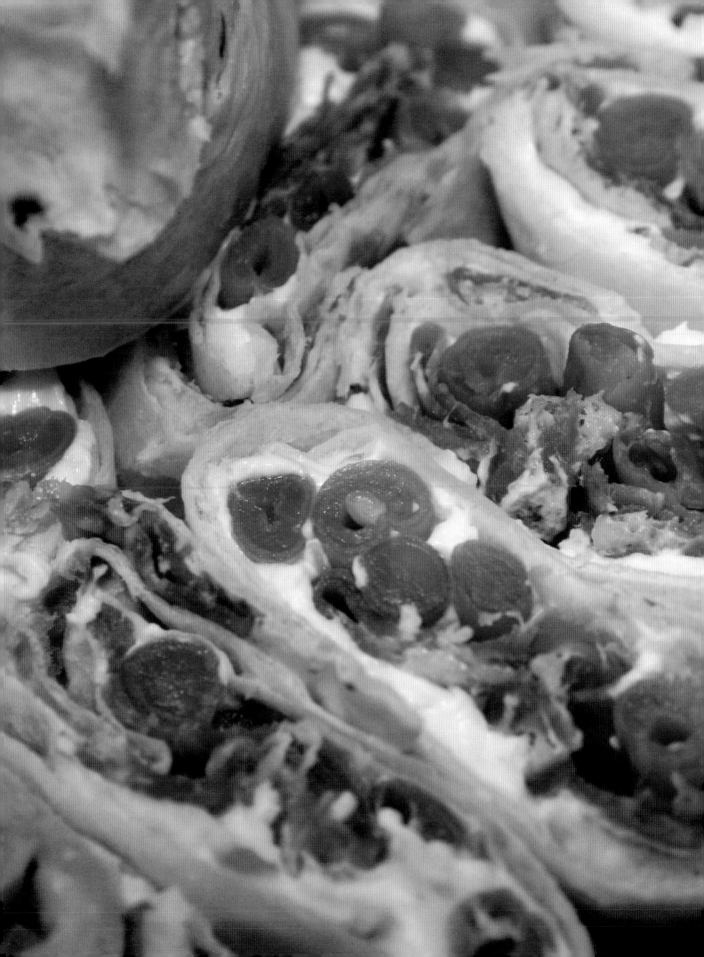

Porky Pinwheel Appetizers

Every year around the holidays, the plethora of quaint, "quick and easy" appetizer recipes makes the rounds. I'm not a fan of any recipe that has the phrase "quick and easy" in its description, usually because they use too many canned or pre-packaged ingredients. Also, some of these recipes lack sophistication and complexity; making ham and cheddar "crostini" doesn't rev my engines. When I have an appetizer, I want to come away from that little bite thinking, "Wow, now *that* was an awesome combination of flavors and textures!"

All that said, I have a weakness for those little rollups everyone makes with flour tortilla shells. They almost always have a cream cheese component, and who doesn't like cream cheese besides the lactose intolerant? I decided to take this basic idea and heighten the experience, if you would, to get away from the ranch dip/cold cut routine.

After studying my grocer's gourmet cheese and cured meat offerings, I ended up with four different combinations for the appetizer. Preparation for any of the combinations isn't rocket science. I used the smaller six-inch tortillas for all of the combinations you see here. If you're using bigger tortillas, you'll need to increase the ingredients. To ensure a good texture for these little bites, use good, thin, fresh flour tortillas rather than the thick mass-produced fare in your grocer's refrigerated case.

SALAMI AND FRESH BABY SPINACH

½ cup of cream cheese
¼ cup Italian oil and vinegar dressing
   (creamy is also okay)
2 six-inch tortillas

½ cup of fresh baby spinach, chopped fine
12 to 15 very thin slices of high-quality
   peppered salami

INSTRUCTIONS

1. Blend your cream cheese and dressing. Spread half of this mixture on each tortilla, covering the entire face less a quarter-inch at the edges.

2. On one half of each tortilla, evenly spread out half the chopped spinach. Lay six to eight salami slices on top of the spinach, then roll up the tortilla from the ingredient end toward the cream-cheese only end, then slice.*

SOPPRESSATA, WHITE BALSAMIC AND GRUYERE, AND GREEN BEANS

1 dozen green beans
¼ cup Gorgonzola and White Balsamic Salad
    dressing (Cindy's Kitchen of Brockton brand)

½ cup of cream cheese
2 six-inch tortillas
10 3-inch thin-sliced rounds of soppressata

INSTRUCTIONS

1. Steam your green beans and transfer to an ice bath as soon as they're tender and before they've lost their bright green color. Once cooled in the ice bath, drain and pat the beans dry.

2. Cream together the salad dressing and the cream cheese. Note, this brand of salad dressings and marinades is beyond tasty and comes in dozens of varieties. Spread half the cheese mixture on each of the tortillas over their entire face, leaving a quarter-inch border around the edge uncovered. Lay half the green beans so that they'll be horizontal within the roll, then lay the soppressata slices on top of them. Roll up each tortilla from the ingredient end toward the cream-cheese only end, then slice.*

BACON AND SHARP WHITE CHEDDAR

2 six-inch tortillas
½ cup of cream cheese

1 cup of grated sharp white cheddar cheese
six strips of gently crisp cooked bacon

INSTRUCTIONS

1. Combine the cream cheese and grated sharp white cheddar cheese. This will be chunkier than the other cream cheese mixes. Spread half on each of the tortillas, covering the face but leaving a ¼-inch border around the edge. Lay three strips of freshly cooked and cooled bacon on one half of each tortilla, then roll from the bacon end toward the cheese-only end, being careful not to the let the bacon strip push through the tortillas and tear it, then slice.*

SAUCISSON (GARLIC SAUSAGE WITH WINE) WITH PORT AND BRANDY CHEDDAR AND FRESH BABY SPINACH

1 cup of Snowdonia brandy cheddar cheese, shredded

½ cup of cream cheese

2 six-inch tortillas

10 to 12 thin, half-dollar-sized slices of *D'Aartagnan Saucisson a l'Ail au Vin Rouge***

½ cup of chopped fresh baby spinach

INSTRUCTIONS

1. Blend the grated port cheese with the cream cheese. Spread the cheese mixture across the face of each tortilla, leaving just a ¼-inch border bare at the edges. Lay five to six slices of *saucisson* on one half of each tortilla, followed by half of the chopped spinach. Roll up from the ingredient side toward the cheese-only side and slice.*

*TIP Two notes about assembly. First, spread your cream cheese base across the entire surface of the tortilla, leaving all but a scant quarter-inch of the edge un-smeared. Second, put the other ingredients on just half the tortilla and begin your roll from that side, rolling away from you and into the cream cheese-only side so that side will stick and hold the roll together. Slice off the ends that won't look nice on the serving plate, then slice the roll firmly and decisively in even sections, working as you go to avoid crushing the roll or squeezing out the insides.

**TIP The *D'Aartagnan Saucisson a l'Ail au Vin Rouge* is a ready-to-eat garlic sausage with red wine that is produced by a French brand and made in the US. It tastes like a breakfast sausage minus the heavy fennel presence and with a very smooth and silky texture; it was quite fat rich. I couldn't taste the red wine, but did catch the very subtle garlic enhancement.

If you can't find this particular sausage, do exactly what I did and try this recipe with something new, such as pâté or *foie gras*.

The cheese I chose to mix with the cream cheese comes from the Snowdonia Cheese Company brand, a producer based in Wales. I bought several rounds, including the Ruby Mist, a sharp white cheddar laced with brandy and port. The cheese is gorgeous and ivory white, and it reveals just a hint of port. It makes an excellent pairing with the *saucisson*. If you can't find this brand, any other aged white cow's cheese with wine or even a red fruit like cherries or cranberries will do.

Ricotta-Stuffed Pork and Basil Meatloaf

There are as many ways to make meatloaf as there are hamburgers. Heck, the former isn't really much different than a hamburger at all, save for its size and cooking method.

Meatballs, too, fall into this category of similarity. The other day, I was making a big batch of the ricotta meatballs (page 133), and, due to my spectacular ability to over-buy ingredients, I ended up with a lot of leftover ground pork and ricotta. I also had a fresh bunch of basil on hand, and that allowed me to come up with this recipe. Here's what you'll need:

INGREDIENTS

1 ½ to 2 pounds of lean ground pork (depending on the size if your loaf pan)*

1 large bunch of fresh basil

1 to 1 ½ tablespoon of garlic powder

1 to 1 ½ tablespoon of onion powder

1 to 1 ½ tablespoon of dried oregano

3 large eggs

2 to 2 ½ cups of seasoned Italian breadcrumbs, garlic preferred

2 to 2 ½ cups of fresh ricotta

1 ½ cups of marinara sauce, plus extra for serving

---

*TIP Your ground pork should be as lean as possible. There's nothing like taking a meatloaf out of the oven and finding not only that you need to pour off a cup of grease, but also that your meal for four has shrunk to a serving better suited for two. If you can't find good-quality ground pork or a grind that's lean enough, mix what you can find with really top-end ground sirloin, ground buffalo, or ground grass-fed beef (which tends to be very lean).

INSTRUCTIONS

1. Bring your ground pork to room temperature

2. Mince your basil very fine (I pulse mine in a food processor). Add that and all your ingredients in their totality to the meatloaf mix, except for the ricotta and marinara—add just ¾ to one cup of the ricotta. You will add marinara toward the end. Mix all this by hand until the

ingredients are evenly distributed. I work it like I knead bread, pushing and squeezing until I see bits of basil everywhere. Add another egg or more breadcrumbs as needed. You certainly don't want a meatloaf dripping with egg that will end up as a loaf-shaped frittata, nor do you want one so stiff that you feel like you're working with Play Doh. At this point you can refrigerate the meat mix and come back to it later or get the loaf prepped and into the oven.

3. When you're ready for the oven, get out your loaf pan and spread half the meat mixture in the bottom of the pan, but do so with a bit of a trough in the center and the meat pushed up the sides of the pan. Spoon the remainder of the ricotta into the trough—it's okay if it touches the sides and ends, but the purpose of the shallow trough is to keep as much of the ricotta inside the loaf as possible.

4. Top the ricotta layer with the other half of the meat mixture, but do this gently. Place it easily on the top, working it down the sides and ends if possible to meet the bottom layer of meat, even if you can't pinch them together. Finally, take a cup and a half of marinara and pour it over the top—though not too much that it flows over the sides and makes a mess in the oven (to be safe, set the loaf pan on a jellyroll pan to catch any spills).

5. Set in a 350-degree oven for 50 to 60 minutes. The edges of the loaf should show through as browned nicely, and the loaf as a whole should be pulled away from the sides of the loaf pan. If it looks a little pink or produces juices that aren't clear, stick it back in the oven for 10-minute increments until the juices are clear and you've attained the pull-away from the pan.

6. When done, let the loaf set on a cold stovetop or trivet for 10 minutes. You can drape it with a clean kitchen towel or tent it with foil if service is imminent. After this resting period, pour off any of the rendered liquid fat, then slice carefully and serve.

7. I like to lay this loaf out in slices on a platter, then ladle over some extra hot marinara sauce.** A spinach salad on the side and a fresh chianti are all you need to complete the picture.

**TIP   An alternative to the extra marinara sauce at service would be to spoon on some fresh pesto sauce. However, I don't like using it as a topping for the meatloaf during baking, as the olive oil makes everything little two greasy, what with the rendered fat from the cooked meat and all. Same goes when you mix pesto into your meat before cooking. That can and often does work beautifully with meatballs and mashed potatoes, but it's too much oil when used in a contained baking utensil like a loaf pan. Oh, one other place it does work really well? Mix a little pesto into your mayo if you like meatloaf sandwiches the next day. It makes a wonderfully zesty addition to a cold meatloaf sandwich made from this recipe.

Roasted Tomato Stew with Italian Sausage and Tortellini

When I moved to Connecticut in the middle of 2014, I discovered my new go-to grocery store, a pretty high-end family-owned establishment. It had an excellent produce section, replete with a wide variety of local and locally organic vegetables, including bins of locally grown tomatoes of all sizes and varieties, from blood-red cherries and plump squat Romos to fire-engine scarlet beefsteaks (and especially the famed New Jersey tomatoes, most of which are a resurrected strain of Romapo and are some of the most mouth-watering tomatoes I've ever sunk my teeth into). All were spectacular in flavor and I couldn't get enough of them.

Luckily, tomato season in the Northeast lasts well into the months when the greenery starts to give way to gold and amber. These are the first days when you yearn for something more filling and hearty than the light table fare of the summer.

This recipe uses a lot of tomatoes. Do choose a variety of tomatoes for this soup—they all have different sugar and acidity levels—and make sure they have a deep, true color to them and are fully ripe.

INGREDIENTS

2 pints of cherry tomatoes
6 Roma tomatoes
6 large beefsteak tomatoes or other large, on the vine tomatoes
1 can of peeled whole tomatoes
Olive oil
Salt and white pepper to taste

2 tablespoons of crushed garlic
4 to 6 cups of chicken stock
1 teaspoon of cayenne pepper
1 ½ to 2 pounds of sweet Italian sausage
1 large bunch of basil
1 20-ounce pack of fresh cheese tortellini (like Buitoni)

1. Take the larger tomatoes and either halve or quarter them, using a paring knife to remove the tough bit where the stem had been. Once cut, spread them in a single, tightly packed layer in two medium-sized gratin dishes; one large roasting pan will also work. Leave the cherry tomatoes whole, filling in the gaps between the larger wedges. Drizzle with extra virgin olive oil and sprinkle with sea salt. (If you love garlic, you can stick peeled garlic cloves in between the tomatoes and roast the garlic, too). Roast the tomatoes at 365 for an hour to 90 minutes, until the cherry tomatoes have burst, the larger wedges are wilted down, and there's quite a bit of bubbling juice in the pan. Remove and let cool on the counter or stovetop.

2. While the tomatoes are cooling, warm a couple tablespoons of olive oil in a stockpot on medium low and slowly cook your crushed garlic. Stir frequently so it doesn't burn, but cook until the garlic turns a light to medium brown and smells heavenly. Turn the burner off.

3. Add the tomatoes and garlic in batches of two to three cups with a cup of chicken broth to a blender and pulse until smooth, then run the blender on low for 30 seconds and then high for the same. What you're looking for is a completely homogenous look—no pieces, no chunks, no different shades of red. You can also put the roasted tomatoes into a stockpot along with the chicken stock and use a handheld stick blender (if you do use a stick blender, it might help to blend all the tomatoes first and then add the stock a little at a time, blending as you go).

4. Once the pureed tomatoes and stock have been combined in the stockpot with the browned garlic, add cayenne and salt, and bring the pot to a low boil, stirring frequently and keeping a lid on the pot to prevent spattering. The consistency of your tomato soup should be a little thinner than chili-sauce thick; not tomato juice thin, but more like a really thick Bloody Mary consistency. Thin as you need with a little more chicken broth.

5. While you're bringing the tomato soup base up to a low boil, sauté your sausage in a large pan. I slit each sausage link down its length with a paring knife and turned the loose meat into the pan. Casings are fine when you're going to slice your links for something like a simple sausage and pepper sauté, but too often they get chewy and stringy in a soup, so best to uncase your links or buy uncased sausage.

6. Once the sausage is cooked, use a slotted spoon to add it to the tomato soup. Next, chop your fresh basil—you should have two cups of loosely bunched chopped herbs—and add that in as well. Bring the works to a boil with the lid on and stir frequently, then reduce to low. Taste for salt and pepper, add as needed, cover the pot, and simmer for at least an hour, stirring occasionally.

7. Thirty minutes before serving, bring the tomato soup and sausage up to a slow boil and add in fresh tortellini. Keep at that low boil, stirring to keep the pasta from sticking at the bottom of the pot, for 10 to 15 minutes. Reduce the pot to medium low again for another 10 minutes, stirring occasionally and keeping a lid on the pot. You'll be ready for service when the soup has thickened from the starch in the pasta and you can no longer resist dipping hot buttered garlic bread into the pot.

TIP Being a complete sucker for tortellini, I ended up adding a second 20-ounce package of cheese tortellini to my pot. After dinner the first night, I left the pot on the cold stovetop overnight. I refrigerated the pot the next morning, then spooned the now mostly liquid-less concoction (the larger amount of pasta absorbed nearly all the tomato soup base) into a casserole dish. I poured in a little more chicken stock, just to keep it from sticking to the bottom of the casserole, covered it with aluminum foil, and reheated for an hour in a 350-degree oven. During the last five minutes, I layered on thick slices of soft, buffalo mozzarella, letting them melt to gorgeous gooeyness. Ta-da! Two dishes from one!

Sausage and Brussels Sprouty-Casserole with Cream of Bacon and Mushroom Sauce

Green bean casserole—or greeny-beeny casserole, as I like to call it—is a perennial favorite of Thanksgiving and Christmas tables across the country, and one I favor enough to make all year round, canned green beans and all, 'cause the same dish with fresh green beans just never seems right. I had a craving for it the other weekend and came up with this twist on the usual, using Brussels sprouts. You sprout haters can move on to the next recipe. Here's what you'll need for a generous 9x13 casserole dish:

INGREDIENTS

20 ounces of baby Brussels sprouts
   (about five cups)
2 pounds of parsley and parmesan Italian sausage*
2 6-ounce containers of French's Fried Onions
2 pounds of white button mushrooms

1 pound of bacon
2 tablespoons of flour
2 cups of whole milk
1 tablespoon of pepper
2 cups of shredded Parmesan

*TIP I used a lovely parsley and Parmesan Italian sausage made at my local grocery store. If you can't find such a sausage, either add extra parmesan at the end or go with a mild sweet Italian sausage.

INSTRUCTIONS

1. There are two ways to go about this. You can either steam your Brussels sprouts until they're tender and set them aside while you work on the other components, or you can save the sprouts for last and cook them until almost done, but then be prepared to mix them in immediately with the other ingredients and pop the dish in the oven so it keeps cooking. I steamed mine up front and set them aside.

2. In a deep saucier, sauté your sausage until cooked through, then drain off the majority of the fat and brown the sausage. Remove to drain one last time (leave a bit of rendered fat in the

pan) and toss the sausage with the cooked Brussels sprouts (if you've steamed them first as I did) in a large bowl, along with one canister of French's fried onions. Pour the contents into your casserole dish.

3. Chop your mushrooms finely (though not minutely). I pulsed mine in a food processor a couple times. Set aside.

4. Take a pound of bacon and, without separating the slices, cut the pack into one-inch slices. This is easiest to do when your bacon is refrigerator cold or even partially frozen. Make sure you use a sharp, un-serrated knife and have a firm surface such as a wood cutting board.

5. Add bacon slices to the pan. Do not clean the pan before doing this. Also, you don't need to separate the individual one-inch pieces of bacon. Simply add them to the still warm pan in which you had cooked the sausage and after stirring them with a flat-edged wood spoon for a few minutes, the pieces will separate themselves.

6. When the bacon is starting to crisp, drain all the rendered fat and add your mushrooms. Again, do not clean the pan. The moisture that will render off the mushrooms will help the browned bits stuck at the bottom of the saucier loosen and flavor the mushrooms as they reduce.

7. When the mushrooms have cooked down to a deep brown and are no longer sitting in their own water, sprinkle them with the flour, mix quickly to coat, then slowly add your milk to make a sauce. Finish with the ground pepper and keep on low heat until ready to assemble the dish, adding more milk and stirring periodically to keep the sauce from getting too thick. You want to be able to pour the sauce—somewhere between the viscosity of the milk and sausage gravy.

8. Once you've got it there, quickly whisk in the grated Parmesan cheese and pour it evenly over the sausage mix in the casserole dish, using a table knife gently inserted into the top of the mix at different intervals to help the sauce work its way through and down. Top the casserole with the contents of the second can of French's Fried Onions and insert into a preheated 350-degree oven for 40 minutes. The onions on the top of the dish should be toasty brown and the sauce visibly bubbling along the sides when done.

9. I *loved* this concoction! It had all the flavor dimensions of a greeny-beany casserole, but with far more depth. Serve it as a side dish or as a meal by itself.

Sausage and Noodle Bake with Cannellini Beans and Mozzarella Pearls

As I've noted before, most pasta is nothing more than a vehicle for meat, sauces, and other tasty items. However, as much as I love pasta and a rockin' good sauce, I get the most out of it when I mix the sauce and other components all in one pot with the cooked pasta, and even more so when I make it into a pasta pie. Here's how you can do that with just a handful of ingredients you likely already have in your pantry and fridge.

INGREDIENTS

2 20-ounce jars of your favorite tomato or marinara sauce

2 tablespoon of olive oil

1 large onion, rough chopped

1 ½ pounds of sweet or spicy Italian sausage (about six or seven links)

2 15-ounce cans of cannellini beans

1 32-ounce can of whole peeled tomatoes

8 ounces of long flat pasta, such as fettuccini or linguini

1 tablespoon of salt

16 ounces of fresh, raw baby spinach

1 cup of grated fresh parmesan cheese

2 8-ounce containers of BelGioioso mozzarella pearls

Salt and pepper to taste

INSTRUCTIONS

1. Put a stockpot and a saucier or deep-sided frying pan on the stove. In the stock pot, pour in both jars of tomato sauce and heat on a medium-low flame. Keep a lid on the pot to reduce spatter.

2. In the sauté pan, heat the tablespoon of olive oil and add your chopped onion. Sauté until the onions are translucent, then add your sausage. You can add the sausage links whole and then slice after they've cooked and cooled, or slice the cases open and use the sausage like ground meat.

3. When the meat and onion mixture is cooked, add to the warm tomato sauce via a slotted spoon. Drain the cannellini beans and add them too. Add the can of whole tomatoes including its juice, then raise the temperature so the pot comes to a simmer.

4. Meanwhile, start your pasta. Fill a large stockpot with cold water, adding in the second tablespoon of oil and a tablespoon of salt. Bring to a boil and add your pasta, cooking until al dente. While you're working on the pasta, work the fresh spinach into the simmering sauce. It should take you four batches from a 16-ounce clamshell of spinach leaves to work them into the sauce and wilt them down in volume. Finally, incorporate the grated parmesan cheese.

5. When the pasta is done cooking, drain in a colander and add immediately to the bubbling tomato sauce. Give it a good mix with a wooden spoon, reaching down to the bottom of the pot and lifting and turning without breaking up the pasta strands.

6. In a 9x13 glass or glazed ceramic casserole pan, spoon in half your pasta mixture. Next, drain one of the containers of mozzarella pearls and distribute them evenly across the pasta. Add the rest of the pasta and top with the other container of drained mozzarella pearls. If you have another jar of pasta sauce on hand, you can pour more across the top, but don't drown the mix in so much sauce that it bubbles over and makes a mess in the oven (to be safe, set your casserole on a jellyroll pan to catch anything that might boil over).

7. Set the dish in a 350-degree oven for 45 minutes to an hour, depending on how deep your dish is. It's okay to see some bubbling, but ideally this should be a denser combination after baking than it was when you first mixed it on the stove—but no harm if there's extra sauce. All you'll need then are a few more napkins.

Sausage and White Beans with Shells

White beans slow cooked in chicken stock and garlic and added to pasta shells tossed with parsley is a peasant-simple dish of minimal ingredients that yields a filling and soothing meal. It is one of my favorite winter evening meals. I took that basic dish, changed the method a little, added sausage, and ended up with a still simple dish that was elegant enough to be eaten in a white table-clothed Italan restaurant. Here's what you'll need:

INGREDIENTS

2 tablespoons of butter

1 tablespoon of olive oil

3 tablespoons of crushed garlic

1 pound of mild Italian sausage

⅛ cup of flour

4 16-ounce cans of white or Navy beans

2 24-ounce boxes of chicken broth/stock

16 ounces of large pasta shells*

Salt and pepper to taste

Water as needed

1 small bunch Italian flat-leaf parsley, chopped

*TIP I specified large shells for the pasta. That means the largest of the spoon-sized shells available, not manicotti-sized shells. You want the largest size because the purpose of the shell design is to cradle a scoop of the other ingredients—in this case the whole beans, bean puree, and a bite of sausage. Go with too small a shell and you'll never get this perfect mouthful.

INSTRUCTIONS

1. In a large stockpot, melt butter and warm olive oil over a low flame. Add garlic and sauté slowly, stirring often until the garlic is toasty brown and smells fabulous, about 20 to 30 minutes.

2. While the garlic is caramelizing, brown your sausage in a sauté pan. I took mine and slit the casings down the length of the links to remove the meat from the casings. Add it to a hot sauté pan, breaking it up as it browns into manageable bite-sized pieces.

3. Your sausage should finish cooking around the same time as the garlic. If you've gotten this right, temporarily remove your garlic that is in the stockpot from the flame to prevent over-browning or burning. Turning back to the sausage, if it has rendered off quite a bit of fat, drain most of it, leaving a couple tablespoons in the pan with the meat. Quickly add your flour, stirring steadily with a flat-edged wooden spoon, until the sausage is coated in this makeshift roux and the rendered fat has been absorbed. Don't overcook; you want your roux to stay blonde. Set aside.

4. Add two cans of the white or Navy beans and one 24-ounce carton of chicken stock/broth to the stockpot with the garlic. Bring the pot up to a low simmer, stirring occasionally for 10 minutes or so. At this point you're going to need one of two tools, either an immersion blender of a countertop blender. Puree the beans, garlic, and chicken stock. An immersion blender will produce a gorgeous, custard-colored and silky smooth concoction in a couple minutes. You can accomplish the same thing with a countertop blender, but you'll have to work in batches.

5. Add your sausage to the white bean puree, along with the second 24-ounce carton of chicken stock or broth. Bring to a low simmer, stirring frequently to keep things from sticking to the bottom of the pot.

6. In a second large stockpot, bring a pot of salted water with a tablespoon of olive oil to boil. Cook your pasta until al dente, and not a bit more. Drain and add it immediately to the bean and sausage simmer. Add the remaining two cans of beans, then enough water to cover by at least an inch. Bring the heat up until the stew is gently bubbling across the surface, stirring frequently as you do, then stir in your chopped parsley. Lid the pot and reduce the flame to low. Keep it there, stirring occasionally, until ready to serve.

7. For service, ladle this thick soup into a generous, wide-mouthed bowl, along with warmed slices of an airy, chewy ciabatta-type bread on the side or even an Englsh muffin. The pockets inside these breads work well to scoop up all that bean puree. A nicely oaked and not-to-dry chardonnay helps to complete this lovely dish.

Shepherd's Pie with Whipped Mascarpone Potatoes and Carrots

Shepherd's pie is one of those perennial church social favorites. It was also likely a dish your mom whipped up when ground beef was on sale, this iconic symbol of what one can do with a frozen vegetable medley, a can of Campbell's Cream of Mushroom Soup, a few spuds, and leftover meat. It is economical, filling, hearty, and comforting at the same time.

It's also a little boring. I set out to change that, of course. Here's what you'll need to make a casserole big enough to serve a crowd (one deep 9x13 pan):

INGREDIENTS

2 cups of small new red potatoes, peels on
4 cups of baby carrots
1 tablespoon of melted butter
Generous salt and ground black pepper
2 cups of very sharp white cheddar cheese
2 cups of fresh sugar snap peas
8 medium red potatoes

3 pounds of lean ground pork
¼ cup of flour
3 cups of whole milk
3 cups of heavy cream
1 ½ cups of mascarpone*
3 large eggs

*TIP Confession: the mascarpone was an accident. I never make mashed potatoes without a copious amount of butter, but that day not one pound of butter could be found in my fridge. Instead, I grabbed mascarpone and eggs as a substitute. It turned out to be a genius move—the whipped mashed potatoes and carrots took on an almost custardy texture.

1. I like to roast the vegetables that I intend to use in a recipe, to give the dish a deeper, richer flavor. Put the new red potatoes (these should be very small with the skin on) and two cups of carrots in a large Ziploc freezer bag, along with a tablespoon of melted butter, a couple teaspoons of salt, and a good tablespoon of ground black pepper**. Massage the bag to ensure an even mix, then pour them into a roasting pan and slide into a 375-degree oven until fork tender, about 45 minutes to an hour. Set aside to cool while you work on the other components.

2. While the vegetables are roasting, trim you sugar snap peas. Using a paring knife, slice off one of the sharp ends, then pull out the tough string that runs down the spine of the pod. Put the trimmed peas in a large mixing bowl and add the roasted potatoes and carrots once they've cooled.

3. Preheat your oven to 350 degrees. Start a large saucier and a stockpot on the stove. Peel and quarter the medium red potatoes and add to the stockpot as well as the remaining two cups of baby carrots. These will become your mashed topping, so bring the pot to a boil until both vegetables are fork tender. Do leave some firmness to the potatoes. The carrots will likely be tender before the potatoes are cooked, and that's okay; this will allow them to incorporate better into the mash. When the vegetables are done, drain in a colander and set aside.

4. While the carrots and spuds are boiling, brown the ground pork in the deep-sided saucier. Most shepherd's pies call for ground beef, but ground pork gives a much more tender bite between the teeth, and its milder taste lets the flavors of the roasted vegetables and fresh snap peas shine through. This is another place to be liberal with salt and pepper. When the pork starts to brown, remove it to the large mixing bowl holding the sugar snap peas and roasted vegetables via a slotted spoon and toss to combine. Distribute this mix in a large, deep-sided casserole dish.

5. Turning back to the saucier now emptied of ground pork, drain off all but four tablespoons of rendered pork fat and, over a medium flame, whisk flour into the remaining fat to make a roux. There's no need to brown this roux; the intention is to make a white gravy spiked with black pepper, a more agreeable substitute to that tired old can of Campbell's soup you're used to using. Whisk the flour and fat until it starts to blond, adding more flour if you need, then incorporate the three cups of milk and two of the three cups of heavy cream. Start with the milk, adding a half-cup and whisking to blend with the roux, then go to the heavy cream, back to the milk and so on until the quantities have been exhausted. Whisk easily and frequently, but not furiously or constantly, to work your gravy to smoothness and keep it from sticking to the pan. Keep the gravy at a low, gentle bubble. As you add each dose of milk or cream, continue to add salt and pepper (less salt than pepper) to taste.

6. When your gravy is smooth, lid the pan and turn the flame off. Give it a couple minutes and whisk it again at what should be a newer, thicker consistency, then repeat this process. The end product should be a little more viscous than biscuits-and-gravy thick. Pour it over the pork and vegetable mix, using a flat-edged wooden spoon pushed into the mix to allow the gravy to flow down as needed.

7. Using a stand mixer, mash your boiled potatoes and carrots. Add your mascarpone (this will combine easier if it's close to room temperature), whipping to combine, then add the eggs one at a time until they are thoroughly incorporated. Your finished mash should be thick and yet have some lightness to it; it should not be runny. If it looks like it's going to be a little loose after the second egg, skip the third. Finally, add the shredded white cheddar cheese, then just enough salt and pepper to bring out the sweetness of the carrots and the earthiness of the potatoes—the pepper should be far more pronounced.

8. Spoon your mash over the top of the meat mixture in the waiting casserole. Spread it across evenly and cover the filling completely from side to side. Set in your 350-degree preheated oven for at least an hour or up to 90 minutes, depending on how deep your casserole dish is. The mash topping should take on a golden hue, and a table knife inserted at the edge should release fragrant steam. Serve piping hot with a cold Bass Ale or Guinness or a super cold glass of milk.

**TIP Did that tablespoon of pepper for the roasted carrots and potatoes feel like a lot? This is because there are no other spices or herbs used in this recipe. There's a reason for this. Sometimes all you need to make the best steak in the world, especially when it's a prime or restaurant-grade cut, is salt and pepper, and the same thing is true for a simple dish like shepherd's pie. It's not that other herbs or spices wouldn't be complementary, but using salt and pepper only will really bring out the depth in the simple components this dish possesses. Be generous with both, using fresh black pepper more than salt, and taste as you go to avoid going overboard. You're looking for prominence, not dominance.

Slow Cooker Provolone and Asiago Mac-N-Cheese with Lit'l Smokies

I have a weak spot for macaroni-and-cheese. I even own a cookbook devoted strictly to the subject. The only problem with that book is that every time I use it, I end up spending $40 just on the cheese. That's a sure way to go bankrupt, not to mention that it cuts into my Scotch and bourbon budget.

Not long ago, I stumbled across some recipes on Pinterest that claimed you can make mac-n-cheese in the slow cooker with nearly no more effort than dumping all the ingredients into the pot, setting the temperature and time, and showing up at the end with a bowl and spoon.

As I've mentioned, I'm skeptical about recipes that have the words "quick and easy" in them. That being said, when a girl wants macaroni and cheese but can't afford to buy the most expensive ingredients, she breaks down and gives said "quick and easy mac-n-cheesy" recipe a try.

No, it won't have the depth of a dish that uses $40 worth of exotic cheeses, but it *is* soul-satisfyingly tasty. I now make this in several variations, including a few, like this one, with fancier cheeses. Here's what you'll need:

INGREDIENTS

1 package of Hillshire Farm Lit'l Smokies mini pork sausages
1 large onion, rough chopped
2 ½ cups of grated aged provolone cheese
1 ½ cups of grated young asiago
2 cups of whole milk

1 cup of heavy cream
2 cups of chicken stock, plus more on hand
1 12-ounce box of small-tube dried rigatoni pasta
1 8-ounce brick of cream cheese
Roasted julienned red peppers for garnish

1. Heat a sauté pan over medium to medium-high heat. Add the Lit'l Smokies, spreading them out in a single layer. Brown these on all sides so the skin is snappy and crisp. As an alternate to the Lit'l Smokies, go with pork kielbasa that is cut in half and sautéed in the same manner. The important thing here is to go pork so that you have, and I say this seriously, a more adult version of this classic dish. There's a delicateness and a hint of sweetness with pork sausages that you simply can't get with beef or chicken.

2. When the Lit'l Smokies are close to being done, throw in chopped onion and stir. Cook until the onions are translucent, but don't let them brown.

3. Grate your cheeses and toss in a bowl to blend together. I picked a provolone that was a little aged, with a bit of saltiness. It melted quite well and had a tang to its flavor. I chose the asiago specifically because it is a young, soft cheese, and its flavors paired wonderfully with the provolone.

4. Pour milk, heavy cream, and chicken stock into the slow cooker. I use a four-quart Breville Risotto Plus that shares multiple cooking chores, including acting as a slow cooker. It's the right volume for this dish, which will fill it to the top.

5. Add dried pasta; it'll cook on its own, so no need to boil ahead of time. Add half the brick of cream cheese, cut up into cubes, on top of the pasta, then half your cheese mix. Now add in half the sausages and onions, and repeat the layers of what's left to fill the pot. Add more chicken stock if you need to, until it reaches an inch or more above the top of the hard ingredients. Don't fill the slow cooker to the top with liquid, but you also do need to provide enough liquid for the pasta to cook through *and* form a sauce with the cream cheese and cheeses. Lid your slow cooker, set it to low, and leave for four hours. When those first hours are up, take a wooden spoon and stir the pot, adding more stock or milk as needed (based on your preference of how creamy you want to make it) until the pasta is cooked in liquid. It should be done in six to eight hours on the low setting.

6. If you want this dish all to yourself and don't want the kids to get their hands on it, take a jar of roasted red peppers, julienne them, heat them quickly in a sauté pan, and stir them into your bowl of mac-n-cheese at service. I guarantee you that the kids will look at it and go, "Ewww, what's that red stuff in the mac-n-cheese?!"

Smashed and Porked New Potatoes

I am one of those folks who can eat a potato with every meal. Bake 'em, sauté 'em, fry 'em, roast 'em, boil 'em, and any other way you can think of to cook them—I'm in.

Recently I ran across a recipe for roasted and smashed new potatoes, kind of like a take on twice-baked potatoes. They're easy to do:

1. Get three cups of small new potatoes (and by small, I mean smaller than a golf ball). My grocery store carries these bags of baby potatoes in varieties red, white, and red/white/blue. Each bag holds three cups.

2. Spread the potatoes in a single layer, skins on, in a shallow gratin or casserole dish, then drizzle with olive oil and sea salt.

3. Roast in a 350-degree oven until fork tender and remove.

4. When cool enough to handle, place the roasted spuds on a jellyroll pan lined with parchment paper, pressing down on each with a fork to smash and burst them open. You don't have to smash them into thinness, just enough to break the skin and expose the inside.

5. Put them back in the oven for another 30 minutes, until the skins are crispy and the potato "meat" starts to turn golden brown.

Easy-peasy. They're delightful just as they are or with melted butter brushed over them. They also make a great foundation for dressing up with pieces of pork. I came up with a few variations for this recipe, beginning at step 4:

- Smash the potatoes and place them back in the casserole dish or gratin. Sprinkle one pound of chopped, slightly undercooked bacon over the potatoes.* Drizzle a cup to 1 ½ cups of creamy French onion dip over the potatoes, but don't coat them. Set back in the oven for 30 minutes. Superb next to a rare steak.

- Follow the same steps as the first method, but this time substitute the French onion dip with the thickest blue cheese dressing you can find. Again, just awesome with a steak or smoked brisket.

- Sprinkle a couple cups of shredded sharp cheddar cheese over the potatoes, then add the pound of chopped bacon.

- Add a pound of cooked crumbled breakfast sausage to the potatoes after you smash them. After their 30 minutes in the oven, serve with a classic white sausage gravy** ladled over the top for a hearty breakfast dish.

- Take a cup and a half of leftover pulled pork, chop it a bit, and sprinkle it over the potatoes. Drizzle a ½ cup or so of honey mustard dressing over them and pop it back in the oven for 30 minutes.

Really, you can let your imagination run wild. What you want to be mindful of is maintaining the integrity of the twice-baked potato concept. You want those potato insides to respond to the second time in the oven and get browned up. So, not only do you not want to totally smother the smashed spuds with the toppings of your choice, but you also want to make sure that your toppings aren't liquidy or they will reduce down and produce a lot of juice (tomatoes, for instance, would be a poor choice).

*TIP As always, I recommend baking your bacon instead of doing it in the frying pan. Take a large jellyroll pan, line it with aluminum foil, and lay out your strips side by side until the pan is full. Set in an oven at 380 degrees for 19 to 25 minutes, depending on your bacon's thickness and fat content (if you have fatty bacon, pour off the rendered fat halfway through the cooking process, otherwise the bacon tends to boil away in its own grease). When the bacon is done, pour the bacon fat into a vessel and drain the bacon on a plate lined with a paper towel or two.

**TIP Note: Sausage gravy is one of my all-time favorite things, and it's a cinch to make.

1. Sauté a pound of ground breakfast sausage in a deep sauce pan.

2. Remove the cooked sausage with a slotted spoon and drain on a plate lined with a paper towel.

3. Pour off all but a ½ cup of the rendered sausage fat, reserving it for use later in another dish.

4. On a medium burner, add a ¼ cup of all-purpose flour to the hot fat, whisking to combine into a blonde paste. Keep whisking until it starts to turn golden, then add two cups of whole milk at room temperature.

5. Continue to whisk to incorporate the flour and fat roux into the milk over medium heat, being careful not to let the milk scald.

6. Add back in your cooked sausage as the gravy starts to thicken, adding more milk (up to two more cups) to achieve your desired thickness. Too thin? Add a little more flour, whisking thoroughly to avoid flour lumps, making sure to get to the bottom of the pan.

7. Lid the pan, reduce the burner to low or turn it off, and let sit for five minutes. The sauce will thicken further during this time, so whisk it one more time and serve.

Smoked "Pulled Pork" Meatballs

Weeks of seemingly unending sub-zero temperatures, the "Polar Vortex," and a February that is light years away from spring, you can get a little cabin crazy. Not only does that mean I'm darn tired of pulling on 82 articles of clothing to walk the dogs, but I'm also craving anything that reminds me of sunshine and warmer months. Most recently, that craving involved pulled pork.

I thought about hitting up the butcher for a Boston butt, but one glance at the temperature forecast for the weekend told me it wouldn't cook correctly anyway (my butts take 12 to 15 hours during good weather). Still, I didn't want to give up on making something porky and barbecue.

Since my pulled pork isn't an ingredient-intensive endeavor beyond a brining and a dry rub and/or sauce, I decided to go the same route with meatballs. What I really wanted was a succulent, flavorful meatball that let the sauce shine through, without any herbiness I'd normally put in a meatball for a spaghetti or a soup. Here's what you'll need:

INGREDIENTS

2 ½ pounds ground pork
2 cups garlic seasoned breadcrumbs (homemade, if possible, described below in step 1)
2 tablespoons crushed garlic
1 cup finely diced onions

1 cup finely diced celery hearts
Generous sprinkling of salt
Your favorite barbecue sauce
Disposable aluminum cooking pan, about 6x9

INSTRUCTIONS

1. Let your ground pork come to room temperature in a large mixing bowl. While that's happening, take half-loaves of any bread you may have, break them into pieces, and scatter them on a large jellyroll tray or cookie sheet. I used a half-loaf of sourdough bread and a half-loaf of soft Italian bread but you can use whatever you like (I think a rye loaf with caraway would be good since caraway goes well with pork). Sprinkle the bread chunks with a little garlic salt. Pop the tray in a 350-degree oven until the bread goldens, about 25 minutes. You can hit the tray briefly with a broiler if you want to get it crunchy. Remove and set on a counter trivet to cool.

2. Once your bread pieces are cool enough to handle, dump them into a food processor and pulse until you have a uniform crumb. You can add a little more garlic powder if you like while you're pulsing.

3. Add your newly made breadcrumbs, crushed garlic, chopped onions, celery hearts, and a good sprinkling of sugar to the room-temperature pork, mixing by hand until combined.

4. Form your meatballs. I made mine fairly large, about half as big as a golf ball. I laid them in the aluminum cooking tray, each touching the next to the side, but with a bit of a gap between one row and the next. If you pack the meatballs together tightly, the smoke will be imparted into all sides of the meatballs, which was what I wanted.

5. Once my tray was filled, I made my barbecue sauce.* Combine two cups of apple cider vinegar, a cup of catsup, a quarter-cup of brown sugar, a bit of salt, a heaping tablespoon of crushed garlic, and a generous tablespoon of red chili flakes in a small saucepan and heat until bubbling, then run it in a blender until smooth. Pour some of your sauce over the meatballs, but do *not* drown your meatballs in sauce.

6. Slide the pan into the smoker. I used apple wood as the tinder and set the smoker to 235 degrees, hotter than I'd normally run because it was winter. I doused a second batch of smoke after the first 90 minutes, and the smoker was holding between 220 and 225 degrees. Because of the extreme cold, I let the meatballs go five hours. Due to the high fat content of the pork and the saucing, the meatballs didn't dry out.**

7. Remove the pan and cut one in half to make sure that the inside is just a half-shade of pink. The outside should have a beautiful, delicate smoky crust. I polished off four large meatballs while leaning over the pan, my cravings for summer Southern pulled pork (almost) satisfied.

*TIP I didn't grow up in one of this country's barbecue meccas—Nashville, Carolina, Kansas City—but I did spend 25 years living in Virginia. It was there that I learned about pulled pork as only the South can do it, and I fell in love. I discovered that the reason I'd never really cared for sauced barbecue was because I'd never had Southern barbecue—the vinegary, red-peppered, and mustardy sauces of Virginia and the Carolinas over the sweet molasses, brown sugar, and catsup sauces from Nashville and K.C. Barbecue sauces are like trucks—you either like your sauce sweet and sassy or vinegary and biting, and you'll take your truck either Ford or Chevy, but you'll rarely cross the line from one side to the other. So use whatever you prefer. Make it from scratch or buy it in a bottle.

Soup of Fennel Sausage, Roasted Mushrooms, Red Bell Peppers, Quinoa, Chia, and Orange

For the past couple years, I have resisted the trend of using old-world grain quinoa (just as I have kale). I remember the wheat-grass craze a couple decades ago. Blech. Fat-free potato chips? Never. The 2014 obsession of putting every last meal, drink, or snack in a Mason jar I also ignored, and I'm quite thankful I wasn't old enough to feel I had to indulge in things encased in aspic or the fondue nuttiness of the seventies.

Which brings me to quinoa. I waited patiently for this one to go away, but the food industry has shown remarkable persistence in its ongoing promotion of this old-world grain. Online and print magazines, not to mention social media feeds, seem to revere quinoa like a four-year-old who just can't let go of the tattered blanket he's had since infancy.

So why did I cave? Well, inspiration strikes in strange places. I was in Las Vegas for a trade show early in the winter of 2015. I had a morning event to attend and the wakeup call was so early that I had room service send up breakfast—a bowl of quinoa porridge laced with orange peel, a bit of brown sugar, and a cranberry sauce reduction. My first spoonful utterly changed my mind about the grain. I wondered why I'd ever eaten oatmeal when this wonderful, nutty, deeply flavored thing called "quinoa" was available. I was an instant convert.

This recipe is a spin on mushroom and barley soup, with quinoa instead of barley. It's based on a fabulous fennel and cracked black pepper sausage I got from my butcher and my memory of that wonderful porridge in Las Vegas. Here's what you'll need.

INGREDIENTS

1 ½ pounds of fennel sausage
2 pounds of white button mushrooms
3 good size red bell peppers
3 tablespoons of truffle olive oil
2 teaspoons of truffle salt
¾ stick of butter
2 large sweet onions
Sugar to taste
1 teaspoon crushed red pepper

⅓ cup of flour
24 ounces of chicken stock
Water as needed
2 teaspoons of fennel seed (optional)
2 teaspoons of black peppercorns (optional)
1 cup of quinoa (preferably red)
2 teaspoons of orange peel
1 cup of orange juice
½ cup of chia seeds

INSTRUCTIONS

1. Right off the bat, you have to get the sausage right—there should be a dominant fennel flavor to it. Everyday breakfast sausage is your best bet if you don't have a butcher that does custom sausage making. A mild Italian sausage might work, but not if it leans heavily on oregano and garlic. If you have any other mild sausage that stays away from the garlic/oregano profile, toast a couple teaspoons of fennel seeds and black peppercorns in a sauté pan, then grind them up (I keep a spare coffee bean grinder just for this purpose alone) for use in the soup. Break up your sausage by slitting the link casings and removing the meat inside. Brown the meat in a sauté pan to bring out its spice profile.At this point, do *not* add the toasted fennel and black pepper blend to the cooking sausage as you'll lose most of it in the rendered fat. When the sausage is cooked, remove from the pan with a slotted spoon and drain on a paper towel-lined plate.

2. While the sausage is cooking, roast your mushrooms and red peppers. Slice the mushrooms in half, put them in a large plastic container, toss them with truffle olive oil and truffle salt until evenly coated, and spread them in an even layer in a large jellyroll pan. Take your peppers and remove the tops and seed pods, and cut them in half. Place the halves skin side up in a gratin dish, drizzle them with truffle olive oil, and sprinkle them with sea salt. Put both the mushrooms and peppers in a 350-degree oven for close to an hour and roast together. The mushrooms should be greatly reduced in size with brown mushroom liquid in the pan, and they should smell heavenly when done. The peppers' skins should shrivel and start to blacken here and there. Remove them and cool. Give the peppers a rough chop and set them aside with the mushrooms.

3. For the soup base, take half the butter allotment and melt over medium-low heat in a stock-pot. Chop your onions finely (about 1 ½ cups) and add them, then add sugar, crushed red pepper, and a pinch or two of salt. Sauté the onions at this low temperature, stirring frequently to prevent burning, until the onions are nicely browned.

4. Add the rest of the butter to the pot and whisk in flour for a quick roux. Whisk fairly constantly for about five minutes, giving it a chance to brown a bit. Pour in your stock and a cup of water, then add the mushrooms only. Bring to a low simmer, stirring frequently, for 15 to 20 minutes. What you're doing is re-plumping those roasted mushrooms and letting them flavor the stock without interference from the other ingredients. Taste the stock at the end of 20 minutes; it should have a very rich and smooth texture with a prominent mushroom taste.

5. Now add your chopped roasted peppers and sausage, along with more water to cover by a couple inches. With the burner at medium, stir until the roux is incorporated, the soup base thickening consistently from top to bottom of the pot. If you're using the toasted fennel seed and black pepper combination, now's the time to add it in, stirring to distribute.

6. Leave the pot on the stove at a low temperature, and lid and stir occasionally for about an hour. Add the quinoa and turn the flame up, bringing the soup to an easy bubbling, stirring frequently to prevent the grain from sticking to the bottom.

7. The dish could be done at this stage, but to enhance it, I added orange peel and orange juice since orange goes well with fresh fennel and pork. You're looking to add the *essence* of orange to the dish; it shouldn't dominate and detract from the soul-satisfying depth of the ingredients already in the pot.

8. Next, add the chia seeds to impart a nutty flavor. Because of the tender, almost barley-like bite they give when they've absorbed liquid, chia seeds make a nice pairing with the quinoa.

9. This, by far, is one of the best soups I have ever created. It reminds me of ordering a specialty soup at a restaurant, one with ingredients you wouldn't normally have thought to combine, and walking away thinking, *Wow, I wish I could make that at home.* Definitely one to sweep dinner guests off their feet with and surefire fare for a mid-winter candlelight dinner next to a roaring fire.

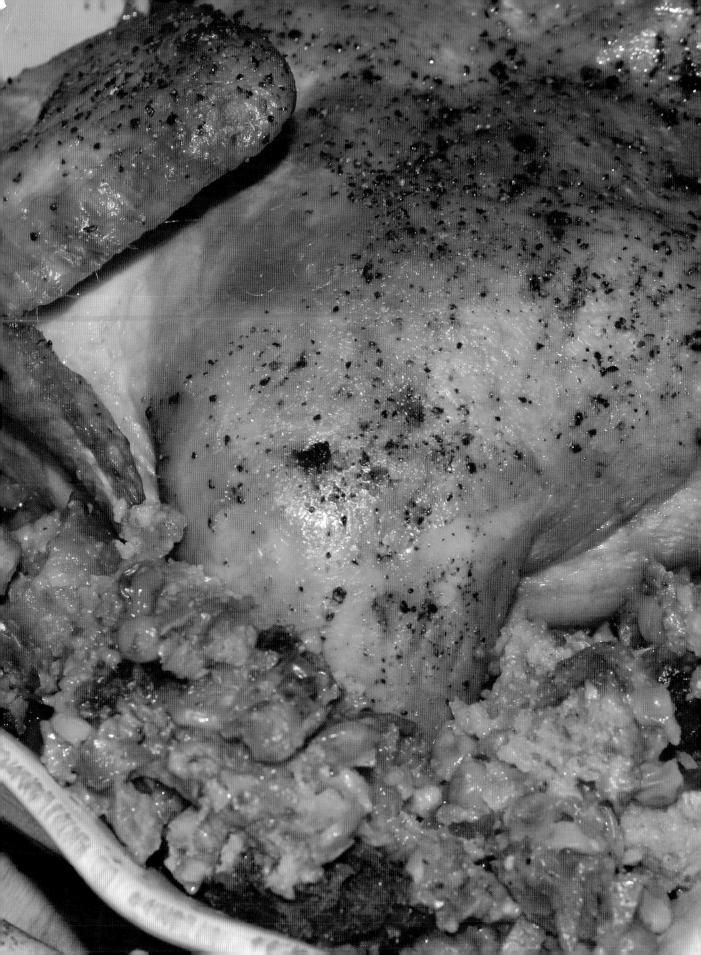

Sourdough and Sausage Stuffing with Sweet Peas

I make stuffing from scratch throughout the year. It's a nice changeup from rice, pasta, and potato side dishes, and you can make it a hundred different ways.

One thing I've discovered is that sausage can make nearly any creation better. I'm not even talking fancy sausage; more often than not, I use Jimmy Dean's every day breakfast sausage. I came up with this simple stuffing as a perfect side to roasted spatchcocked chicken. Here's what you'll need:

INGREDIENTS

5-6 cups of cubed fresh sourdough bread
2 pounds of Jimmy Dean breakfast sausage
2 large sweet onions, chopped medium
2 cups of frozen sweet peas

1 ½ to 2 cups of chicken stock
3 eggs
Salt and pepper to taste

INSTRUCTIONS

1. Hand tear or cut a loaf of sourdough bread until you have five to six cups. Spread the pieces in a single even layer on a cookie sheet or jellyroll pan and place in a pre-heated 350-degree oven until toasted a light golden brown, probably 45 minutes. Some people leave their bread out overnight to go stale and skip the toasting, but I think my way adds more flavor to the stuffing and keeps the bread from turning to mush when you add the liquid. When the cubes are toasted, remove from the oven and allow to cool to room temperature before putting in a large mixing bowl.

2. While the cubes are toasting, brown your sausage, breaking it down to a consistent crumble as you go. When done, remove the sausage with a slotted spoon and add to the cooled bread cubes.

3. Pour off most of the excess fat from the sausage, leaving a couple teaspoons behind. Add chopped onions and sauté on medium until the onions are translucent and have absorbed most of the sausage fat, but take them off the heat before they start to brown. Add them to the sausage bread cubes, then add in your frozen peas. Frozen peas hold up

both in shape and bite when cooked in a stuffing like this, tossed with pasta, or added to a soup, whereas canned and even fresh peas will simply disintegrate.

4. Heat your stock to steaming. Start by pouring one cup of stock over the mix of stuffing ingredients, quickly mixing it with a flat-edged wooden spoon to dampen the toasted bread uniformly. Add more stock as needed until you have everything moistened consistently; you may not need the full two cups. Do not add so much stock that you end up soaking the bread. Sprinkle on a couple pinches of salt and pepper and give it all a quick stir to distribute.

5. Whisk three eggs and pour a little over the stuffing, mixing with a spoon or gently combining by hand. As it is with the stock, you may not need all three eggs. You just want a little bit of binder so that the stuffing doesn't fall apart on the fork.

6. Spread your stuffing evenly in a casserole dish; I used a deep 9x13. Do not press it down and pack it. I spatchcocked my chicken, rubbed it liberally inside and out and under the skin with sea salt and ground black pepper, and laid that on top of the stuffing base to roast at 365 degrees for an hour, or until the skin is golden brown and juices from the chicken run clear. You can stuff a whole chicken and bake the remainder of the stuffing in a casserole dish, but I like it under the spatchcocked chicken as the stuffing gets to absorb the juices from the chicken as it roasts. This scratch-made stuffing, simple in its composition and light on the fork, was a pleasure on the tongue, with a bit of zing from the sourdough and a buttery richness from the sautéed sausage.

Thrice-Layered Chorizo with Manchego

I often eat very simply, especially in the evenings after a trip to the gym, and often for breakfast when I want something filling but can't muster the energy to whip up pancakes. I am a particular fan of rice and beans. In fact, when I make rice for an evening meal, I always make double what I need so I can have rice with refried beans, black beans, chili beans, black-eyed peas, softly fried eggs, and a little hot sauce the next morning. I usually tend to mix the rice *into* the beans and other ingredients, but with this recipe, I ended up leaving it alone, in a singular layer, and it worked out perfectly. Here's what you'll need.

INGREDIENTS

1 tablespoon of bacon fat or olive oil
1 large sweet onion
1 pound of hard chorizo
3 cups of hot cooked rice (Jasmine preferred)

2 16-ounce cans of refried beans, or about 2 cups of homemade
1 16-ounce jar of Frontera red enchilada sauce
1 16-ounce wedge of Manchego cheese

INSTRUCTIONS

1. I used chorizo from the brand D'Artagnan, which was well-spiced and smoky. Heat a large braising pan over medium-high heat and melt the bacon fat. Add the onion, diced small, and the chorizo, sliced into 1/8-inch rounds. Sauté together until the onions are translucent and start to take on some color, and the chorizo browns up and sizzles. Meanwhile, cook jasmine rice in a rice cooker.

2. When the sausage is done, scoop refried beans across the top. Reduce the temperature to below medium and lid the pan. After five minutes check the pan to see if the canned beans are more pliable. Instead of mixing them in, smooth them over the top of the onions and chorizo. Spread on two cups of rice, again resisting the urge the mix it all together. Lid the pan, reduced the burner, and let the convection in the pan allow the creamy refried beans to ooze down around the chorizo.

3. Check the pan after five minutes, then add the enchilada sauce, pouring it over the rice and smoothing it to cover with the back of a spoon, but, again, not mixing it in. Next, add triangles of Manchego cheese, reduce the heat to low, and put a lid on the pan. After five minutes, turn the burner off and let the pan sit, covered, for another 10 minutes before serving, which will help the bottom unstick from the pan.

4. If you're successful you should be able to cut into the dish with a spatula and serve it up like pie, the layers clearly defined to make for an attractive presentation. More importantly, I loved the way the flavors of each component stood out *and* worked together. Serve up chilled avocado and tomato slices and a cold *cervezas*.

Wildly Sweet Cornbread and Sausage Stuffing

I often wonder why stuffing is rarely made more than twice a year. Potato sides aren't any harder or easier, and while warm, buttered bread is a welcome addition to a meal, stuffing can bridge the gap between protein and vegetable more than it does.

One of the dishes my family always loved from me during Thanksgiving was a sausage-based stuffing that also used chicken-flavored Rice-a-Roni (don't laugh, it's awesome). Recently I had the occasion to roast fresh duck I had killed myself, wild and on the wing in some flooded timber in Arkansas, for good friends. The ducks were calling out for wild rice, and that's how I came up with this lovely dish.

INGREDIENTS

8 large cornbread muffins or mini cornbread loaves

2 cups of wild rice

1 large sweet onion or 10 green onions

1 ½ cups of chopped dried apricots

2 pounds of Jimmy Dean breakfast sausage (either regular or sage)*

1 ½ cups of chicken stock

Salt and pepper to taste

*TIP You can use any sausage you like, but I promise you that Jimmy Dean ground breakfast sausage works across a range of dishes. When the spices of Italian, chorizo, bratwurst or other sausage just don't mesh with a dish and you need sausage, Jimmy Dean breakfast sausage does the trick. Do *not,* on the other hand, use links, patties, or any kind of pre-cooked breakfast sausage, and for gawd's sake don't even think about using that horrible stuff called "turkey sausage."

1. Break apart the corn muffins and spread the chunks out on a large cookie sheet. Set them in a preheated 350-degree oven, going about 20 minutes until the edges start to brown and the bread has lost its moistness. While the cornbread is toasting, cook two cups of wild rice.

2. Chop your green onions (whites and greens) and apricots (small dice, about a ¼ inch to ½ inch) and set aside.

3. Sauté the sausage until brown, and remove from the heat. In a small saucepan, bring the chicken stock to a quick boil.

4. Put your toasted cornbread in a large mixing bowl. Pour half the chicken stock over the top and toss with a fork to combine. Add more stock a little at a time, gently tossing so that all of the toasted cornbread is moistened, but not soggy.

5. Add the sausage to the cornbread. If your brand rendered out a lot of fat, use a slotted spoon. Add the hot wild rice, chopped green onions, and chopped apricots, using a flat-edged wooden spoon to combine. Be gentle—you only want to distribute the ingredients evenly, not reduce the cornbread to crumbs.

6. Spread the stuffing mixture into a large buttered or non-stick casserole dish and bake, covered with foil, for 30 minutes in a 350-degree oven. Remove the foil and bake for another 15 to 20 minutes, until the top has a nice toasty crust.

7. This is a great side for fowl and pork dishes. For the ducks I made the night I created this stuffing, I spatchcocked four birds, seasoned them with salt and pepper, then covered them each with about five strips of bacon (wild ducks don't have any fat on them, and the bacon is necessary to keep them from drying out). This stuffing is a perfect side to roast chicken, great for stuffing fat, thick pork chops, and good for stuffing a butterflied pork or venison loin. The sausage is succulent, the cornbread and wild rice sweet and filling, and the tangy apricots a divine foil to the sharp green onions.

You Say Tomato, I Say Tomatillo Chili

Like barbecue, chili has various camps of flavor followers. You have those that rely on sugar and super sweet tomatoes, others that test the limits of the Scoville heat scale, and a whole lot of in between. But unless you're making a white chili with chicken, most chilis are red. I set out to change that with two recipes that embrace the green things in life. You'll find the recipe for "Chili Gone Green" on page 116, and here's what you'll need for this fabulous tomatillo version:

INGREDIENTS

2 pounds of soft chorizo

1 large sweet onion, chopped medium-fine

2 large ancient sweet red peppers, chopped medium-fine

4 large poblano peppers, chopped medium-fine

4 medium red tomatoes, quartered

6 to 8 full-size campari tomatoes, whole

6 to 8 medium tomatillos, husks removed and cut in half

1 6-ounce can of tomato paste

2 tablespoons cumin

2 teaspoons red chili flakes

1 teaspoon cayenne

1 tablespoon roasted ancho chili powder

Salt to taste

3 tablespoons crushed garlic

INSTRUCTIONS

You can make this all in one pot if you like, but a slow cooker also works if you're short on time and don't want to watch the pot. In fact, you can take fifteen minutes in the morning while you're working on your second cup of coffee to get this rolling in the slow cooker, and you'll have dinner when you get home.

Stockpot Method

Start by sautéing your chorizo over a medium to medium-high burner. If you can't find a chorizo with good color and spice, Johnsonville's links or the Ranchero/Cacique brand are also pretty good.

When the chorizo is cooked, stir in chopped onion, stirring occasionally until translucent, about 10 minutes. Add the chopped peppers, stirring occasionally until they begin to soften, 15 to 20 minutes. Add your tomatoes, tomatillos, and tomato paste next (remember to remove the husks from the tomatillos and the hard stem parts from all the fruit). Give it 30 minutes on medium at a low simmer to break down the tomatoes and tomatillos, then add in your spices and garlic, lid the pot, and bring to a happy bubble. Leave it there for a couple minutes, stirring to prevent burning in the bottom, then lid the pot, lower the flame to medium-low, and simmer until you're ready to serve, stirring occasionally.

Slow Cooker Method

Sauté your chorizo. Pour off extra grease or use a slotted spoon to transfer the meat to a stockpot, then add in all your other ingredients. Give it a good stir to distribute everything evenly, then lid your slow cooker and set it to low for at least six hours.

The tomatillos add a refreshing tartness to this chili and is a nice change from the straight-up red tomato dishes. As a garnish, I like to add a dollop of sour cream and a handful of shredded Monterey Jack cheese or *queso fresco*, instead of going with the staple accoutrement of cornbread. Make this one during the summer with herbed and buttered corn on the cob roasted in its own husk on the grill.

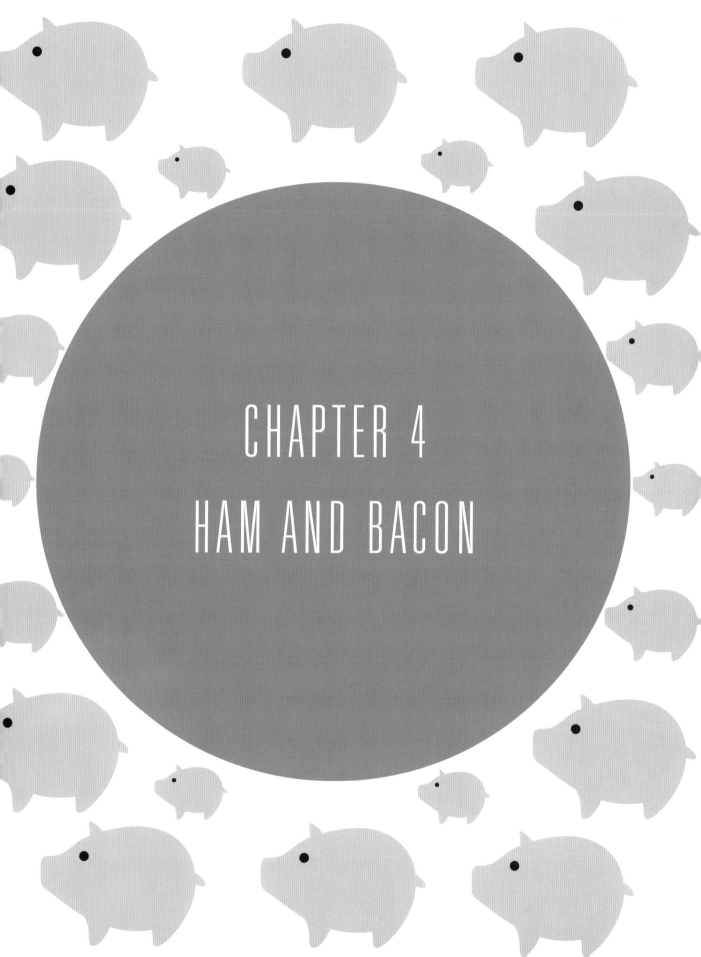

CHAPTER 4
HAM AND BACON

Bacon and Roasted Corn Salsa

Nothing speaks to the sweetness of summer like sweet corn. And nothing complements sweet corn like bacon. Put the two together with a few more things and you have a chip dip unlike any other. Here's what you'll need to make a couple cups:

INGREDIENTS

8 to 10 ears of fresh corn
1 pound of bacon
½ stick of butter, melted
1 teaspoon of ground cayenne pepper
½ teaspoon of salt

Half of one red onion, diced fine
1 jalapeño pepper, chopped fine
6 green onions chopped, both whites
  and greens
1 tablespoon of mayonnaise

INSTRUCTIONS

1. Soak the corn ears in a large pot of cold water for an hour.

2. Cook your bacon in a 380-degree oven for 17 to 25 minutes on a foil-covered jellyroll pan (page 27–29).

3. Melt the butter and combine with cayenne and ½ teaspoon of salt. Peel back the green leaves on each cob but don't remove. Remove the silk, then brush each cob with the butter mixture, pulling the leaves up around the cob. Place the cobs, three to four in a batch, on a sheet of aluminum foil, bringing the foil up around them but not totally closing them in, i.e., you want to leave the top open to vent steam.

4. When your bacon is done, remove the tray and slide in the corn. Roast at that temperature for 20 minutes.

5. Drain your bacon on a plate lined with paper towels. When it is cool, chop roughly and put in a mixing bowl. Do the same with your other vegetables.

6. When the corn is cool enough to handle, cut the bottoms off the cobs, stand each on this newly flattened end, and remove the roasted kernels with a sharp knife, slicing from top to bottom. Add the corn to the bacon and vegetable mix, toss with mayonnaise if you like, and serve up with the best tortilla chips you can find.

Bacon and Cheddar Garlic Smashed Potatoes

I've remarked before that I'm a meat-and-potatoes kind of girl, despite my proclivity to experiment in the kitchen. When you get right down to it, a burger and fries, meatloaf and smashed spuds, and steak and a Russet is where it's at for me.

I whipped up these smashed and rebaked taters to go with the bacon-wrapped mini meatloaves, but they can go with any dish at any time. Here's what you'll need:

INGREDIENTS

3 pounds of yellow gold potatoes (thin skinned and waxy type)
3 tablespoons of sautéed garlic (directions below)
1 cup of sour cream

2 cups of shredded sharp cheddar cheese
1 stick of butter
2 cups of bacon, diced fine
Salt and pepper to taste

INSTRUCTIONS

1. Peel your potatoes and cut them into even chunks, around 1 ½ inches. Put them in a large stockpot of lightly salted water and bring to a boil. Keep at a low boil until the potatoes are fork tender; don't boil them so far that they fall apart when speared with a fork, otherwise you end up with mush.

2. Meanwhile, heat a couple tablespoons of extra virgin olive oil in a shallow sauté pan just shy of sizzling. Flick wet fingers at it to test—a hiss is good, a popping spatter not so much. Add your chopped garlic, stir quickly to coat in the hot oil, and reduce your burner to quite low. Let it sauté on a low burner until the garlic starts to brown. Low and slow is the key here. Such cooking transforms garlic into something nutty and sweet, with none of the bitterness it has raw. Keep an eye on it and give it a quick stir with a fork every now and again. Once it's a deep gold, remove from the heat.

3. Drain your potatoes and put them in the bowl of your stand mixer. Beat on medium until the potatoes are smooth, but don't beat them into butter-smooth oblivion.

4. Add your garlic, oil and all, and combine, then add sour cream, cheddar, butter (cut your stick of butter into tablespoon chunks so that it melts easily in the hot potato mixture), and finally bacon. Salt and pepper to taste, then pour into a casserole dish and pop it into a 350-degree oven for 45 minutes to an hour. You can hit it with the broiler at the end for extra crust on the top and give your steaks a chance to rest from off the grill at the same time. Dinner is served!

Bacon, Mushroom, and Candied Onion Tart

After a year of cooking bacon for the *Big Book of Bacon*, I left it behind and moved on to the other cuts. Still, that doesn't mean this ol' girl can't get a hankering now and again.

Once, I baked a sweet onion pie for the winter holidays that disappeared so fast the prime rib roast that went with it stood by looking nearly ashamed. By the time I got around to working on the recipe, my grocer's supply of sweet onions was woeful. I snagged a bag of organic yellows instead, a pound of sliced mushrooms, and came up with this gorgeous dish. Here's what you'll need

INGREDIENTS

2 pounds of bacon
8 to 10 small- to medium-sized yellow onions
¼ cup of butter or bacon fat
½ cup of light brown sugar
½ cup of white sugar
1 pound of small Portobello mushrooms

1 tablespoon of ground black pepper
8 ounces of Kerrygold sweet white
    cheddar cheese*
Dough for one 9-inch pie crust
1 to 1 ½ cups of panko bread crumbs

*TIP I used Kerrygold cheese because this particular blend has a touch of sweetness and a texture that isn't crumbly dry but also lacks the grease other melted yellow cheddars have. If you can't find Kerrygold, go with Cabot's super-sharp white cheddar or another drier aged cheese of the same variety. Even high-quality super-sharp yellow cheeses produce more grease, and with all the bacon in this dish, you definitely want to avoid that.

1. Cook your bacon in a 380-degree oven for 17 to 25 minutes on a foil-covered jellyroll pan (page 27–29) and drain on a plate lined with paper towels. Since you'll need to rotate two pans for this recipe, be sure to pour off the fat from the first batch before you cook the second.

2. While the bacon's cooking, start the onions. Take the ends and the tough outer layers off, then rough-chop them or thin slice them. You should have a minimum of five cups of raw onions.

3. Reserving a tablespoon for the mushrooms, heat either your fresh bacon fat or butter over medium heat in a large, deep saucier or stock pot and add the chopped onions. Throw in ground black pepper and toss to coat the onions evenly with the spice and melted butter.

4. Stirring every few minutes, sweat down your onions. You absolutely want to keep the heat at medium, no more than just a hair above. You want to caramelize the onions, and while they will be dark brown when finished, they will not be fry-browned.

5. When the onions become translucent and get a little tacky as they absorb the fat in the pan and as the water in them cooks out and evaporates, add half quantities of the brown and white sugars. Stirring every couple of minutes, let the onions cook down for another 10 to 15 minutes, then add the remaining sugars and continue in the same vein. Your should have about two to three cups of caramel-brown onions. Transfer to a medium mixing bowl.

6. Melt the remaining butter or bacon fat in the pan where you just cooked the onions. Halve or quarter your baby portobello mushrooms and add them to the hot fat. Sauté until their volume is reduced to less than half and they're starting to. At this point their water will have evaporated from the pan, which is necessary to keeping the finished tart from being soggy.

7. Add the mushrooms to the onions. Finely chop your cooled, finished bacon—I pulsed mine in a food processor for uniformity—and add that next. Taste, adding black pepper as needed; you shouldn't need salt, but adjust as needed to your liking. Finally, shred your cheese and mix it into the cool bacon and onion mix to distribute evenly.

8. Center your pie dough in the tart pan and gently press the edges into the rippled pan edge. If you don't have a tart pan, use a low-sided casserole dish, ceramic gratin, or an everyday glass pie dish. Remember to trim the dough on a rectangular dish so that the height on all sides is even.

9. Preheat your oven to 400 to 425 degrees. Prick the bottom of the raw pie crust all over with a fork. Next, cut a square of parchment paper that goes two or three inches wider than your tart or other pie pan and place the paper over your raw piecrust. Finally, weigh the paper down either with piecrust weights or dried beans. Slide the tart or pie plate into your oven and let

it par-bake about 15 to 20 minutes, just until it starts to golden and brown a bit. Once it's there, take it out of the oven and reduce your oven heat to 375.

10. Pour the bacon mix into your par-baked crust, spreading the mixture evenly and smoothing the top, but not pressing down or compacting it. Top with the panko bread crumbs spread evenly across the surface, then pop into the oven for 45 minutes, until the panko toasts up nicely and the edge of the pie crust is golden brown and no longer raw.

11. This is a very rich dish. Pair a small slice as a side to a hearty steak for dinner or with a fresh salad for a Sunday brunch. Cold beer goes well with it, as does a dry rose wine.

DOUGH FOR 1 NINE-INCH CRUST

1 ½ cups of flour
¼ teaspoon of salt
⅔ cup of butter, lard, or Crisco, very cold
¼ cup of very cold water

INSTRUCTIONS

1. Mix together flour and salt. Cut your fat source into tablespoon-size pieces—your fat should be cold, but not frozen. Using either a fork or a hand-held pastry blender (I prefer the blender), work your fat source into the flour mix until it comes together and resembles a bowl full of tiny peas. Add very cold water, one tablespoon at a time, incorporating it into the fat and flour combination until it starts to resemble dough. Stop as soon as you get to that point.

2. Flour your hands and gently form the ragged dough into a soft ball. Wrap tightly in plastic wrap and place the dough in the refrigerator for at least an hour.

3. To roll out the dough, lightly flour a wood cutting board or Silpat rolling mat and flour your rolling pin. Place your dough in the middle of the mat and roll it out to a 10-inch circle of even depth. Lift gently and transfer to your tart pan or pie dish, trimming the excess dough above the rim and discarding.

Kicked-Up Colcannon

One of the prettiest cookbooks I own is a tome entitled *Elegant Irish Cooking*. As I was leafing through it, I came across a recipe for a dish called "colcannon."

If you frequent an Irish pub or celebrate St. Patty's day with any regularity, you'll be familiar with this simple dish. It seems to be the solution to leftovers from St. Patty's traditional corned beef dinner—well, at least my two favorite components, the potatoes and cabbage. That's all colcannon really is—mashed potatoes combined with cabbage, salt, pepper, butter, and milk. It ranks right up there with mac-n-cheese on the comfort food scale. For this recipe, I changed it up and made good use of some leftover ham. Here's what you'll need to make a large dish to feed a crowd:

INGREDIENTS

4 pounds of waxy potatoes, such as
    Yukon Gold
1 medium head of green cabbage
2 tablespoons of melted bacon fat, melted
    butter, or olive oil
Salt and pepper to taste
4 cups of cooked ham, chopped fine

1 cup of prepared horseradish sauce
½ stick of butter
2 tablespoons of chopped horseradish
    (optional, depending on how zingy you
    prefer your dish)
1 cup of heavy whipping cream
1 medium head of Savoy cabbage

INSTRUCTIONS

1. Peel your potatoes and halve or quarter them to uniform two-inch chunks. Place the chunks in a stockpot of water, bring to a boil, and cook until fork tender. Drain and set aside.

2. While you're cooking the potatoes, core your green cabbage head and slice it into several thin wedges. Place the wedges in a roasting pan, jellyroll pan, or gratin dish, drizzle with melted bacon fat (or butter or olive oil), sprinkle with salt and pepper, and place in a pre-heated 350-degree oven. Roast until the cabbage starts to brown, about 45 minutes, but don't let it lose its pale green color. Remove from the oven and set aside to cool.

3. Chop your ham. If you don't have leftover ham, use a small pre-cooked boneless ham. I actually took my ham in thick chunks and pulsed it briefly in a food processor to break it down. I prefer this to cutting it up with a knife, as the food processor not only gives you a really uniform chop, but also helps break up those strands of inedible connective tissue in boneless.

4. Sauté the ham in a fry pan to sweat off the excess water. The browning also imparts extra flavor.

5. Mash your potatoes in a stand mixer, though you can also do this by hand. Incorporate the horseradish sauce, butter, and the prepared horseradish as you mash, and sprinkle in salt and ground black pepper. Turn the mashed potatoes into a larger mixing bowl.

6. Rough chop your cooled cabbage and add it and your sautéed ham to the potatoes. Add heavy whipping cream and mix thoroughly to distribute the ham and cabbage evenly throughout the mashed potatoes, then spread all of it in a casserole or gratin dish. Set in a 350-degree oven until the top starts to brown, 45 minutes to an hour.

7. For service, simply serve this up piping hot with a cold glass of milk on the side. I had a head of Savoy cabbage on hand, so I cored that, sliced it thin, and sautéed it in butter, alternately stirring and lidding until the cabbage was tender but still bright green. I placed the cabbage in the bottom of a bowl and spooned on a generous scoop of colcannon for an extra dose of veggies. I also ate it for breakfast with a runny-yolked over-easy egg on top.

Leave-the-Chicken-Behind Ham Salad

I do love chicken salad—all those chunks of tender chicken, creamy mayonnaise, crunchy bits of celery, and soft white bread. That's all fine and good, but you can also make ham salad, and it'll be damn good. Here's what you'll need for two or three sandwiches:

INGREDIENTS

2 cups of chopped baked ham
½ cup chopped celery
2 hardboiled eggs

¼ to ½ cup chopped sweet baby gherkins
2 cups of shredded Monterey Jack cheese
½ cup of mayonnaise

INSTRUCTIONS

1. The key to making this better than average is to slice the ham, celery, eggs, and gherkins the same size. They should be finely diced, but not so fine that it's minced to miniscule bits. One caveat: go easy on the gherkins. Some brands are super sweet and they can take over a salad like this. Sample and add more as you need, but you want the gherkins to complement the ham, not take center stage.

2. Put these chopped ingredients in a mixing bowl. Toss gently with shredded cheese using your hands, then carefully fold in mayonnaise until the salad mix achieves a consistency to your liking. I don't mind mine with a extra slather, but I definitely don't want too much mayo. Also, be careful mixing in the mayo; if you're too aggressive, you'll disintegrate the hardboiled egg and make mush out of the salad.

3. You can eat this right away, but 30 minutes in the fridge will set it up and marry everything together. I like mine on good, thick, soft white bread, with cold shredded Romaine lettuce. It is a perfect solution for any leftover holiday hams.

Scalloped Potato and Black Forest Ham Pie with Orange, Lavender, and Rosemary

I could eat scalloped potatoes with just about any meal. That decadent, lusciously good yet oh-so-simple combination of cream, butter, salt, and pepper does something magical when baked around thinly sliced potatoes. This recipe is a version of a scalloped ham and potato pie, with a bit of a step up from the comfort food category. Here's what you'll need:

INGREDIENTS

5 cups of thin-sliced potatoes, waxy-skinned variety (either Yukon Gold or redskin)
¾ stick of butter
2 teaspoons of salt
1 teaspoon of white ground pepper
3 cups of whole milk
2 cups of heavy whipping cream

4 tablespoons of dried orange peel
2 tablespoons of dried edible lavender
Leaves from three to four sprigs of fresh rosemary
1 double pie crust for a nine-inch pie plate
1 ½ pounds thin sliced Black Forest ham (I used Boar's Head brand)

INSTRUCTIONS

1. Peel your potatoes and slice them thin, about 1/8-inch thick. If possible, keep your slices in rounds. Put the slices in a bowl of cold water. Let them sit in the water for 30 minutes to an hour. This will keep the potatoes from turning black due to oxidation, and it also removes some of the starch from the potatoes, which keeps them from gumming up when you cook them.

2. Take a large saucier or wide-mouthed stock pot and melt your butter over a medium flame. When the butter is almost all melted, blot the potatoes dry with a paper towel and lay them in the melted butter. Once you've made one layer that covers the pan, sprinkle on salt and white pepper, then repeat the layer with remaining potato slices, as well as a little more salt and pepper. Using a flat-edged wood spoon, gently stir the potatoes, reaching down from the side to the bottom of the pan and lifting up, mixing the two layers together so they are evenly coated.

3. Add a good measure of milk and half your heavy cream, enough to just cover your potatoes. Sprinkle in orange peel, lavender, and rosemary, and stir gently to combine. Try to leave the slices as intact as possible instead of breaking them into jagged, inconsistent pieces.

4. Lid the pan and stir the pot every couple of minutes to ensure that the dairy isn't scalding and the potatoes are not sticking to the bottom of the pan. The potatoes will cook for close to 30 minutes before they're fork tender. During that time, the milk and cream may become completely absorbed or thickened by the potatoes. You want there to be a little more sauce for the actual pie build, because the baking will once again reduce and thicken the sauce, so add more milk and cream as needed until there's a small quantity of sauce among the potatoes once they're cooked through.

5. Start conservatively with the dried orange peel and lavender, a tablespoon of one and a teaspoon of the other, respectively. Lift the lid to stir the potatoes and taste as you go for hints of orange and lavender, adding more as needed and sprinkling in more salt or ground white pepper to taste until the sauce really wears the *essence* of orange peel and lavender. It should be a more subtle thing on the tongue than a perfume in your nose.

6. Preheat your oven to 375 degrees. Lay your bottom pie crust in your pie dish. You can make this from scratch (recipe below), or cheat and purchase one from your grocer's.

7. Put half the potatoes in the pie dish, covering the bottom crust evenly and nearly to the rim of the pie plate. Lay individual slices of thinly sliced Black Forest ham in folded ribbons around the pie's perimeter. Repeat this process, working around the exposed circle of potatoes in the center of the pie, until the bottom potato layer is completely covered in pretty pink ham. Top this with the second half of the potatoes, mounding them in a hill shape that peaks in the middle. Lay your top crust on top, pinch it down against the edges of the bottom crust, trim excess dough, and crimp your pressed edges to seal.

8. Make three slices across the top dough layer to vent, then set the pie on a jellyroll sheet (in case of spillover), and slip it in the oven for an hour, Remove the pie and let it sit on the counter for 20 minutes.

9. This pie is so lovely, a step up from the ham and potato pie or casserole everyone loves. It makes a superb brunch dish with a light fruit salad on the side, as well as a wonderful dinner with a buttery chardonnay. You will not be able to resist seconds.

DOUGH FOR 2 NINE-INCH CRUSTS

3 cups of flour
½-teaspoon of salt
1 ¼ cup of butter, lard, or Crisco, very cold
⅓ cup of very cold water

INSTRUCTIONS

1. Mix the flour and salt. Cut your fat source into tablespoon-sized pieces—your fat should be cold, but not frozen. Using either a fork or a hand-held pastry blender (I prefer the blender), work your fat source into the flour mix until it comes together and resembles a bowl of tiny peas. Now add in very cold water, one tablespoon at a time, incorporating it into the fat and flour combination until it starts to resemble dough. Stop as soon as you get to that point.

2. Flour your hands, and gently form the ragged dough into a soft ball. Divide the ball into two balls, smooth any edges from the divide, and wrap each dough ball tightly in plastic wrap and place in the refrigerator for at least an hour.

3. To roll out the dough, lightly flour a wood cutting board or Silpat rolling mat, and flour your rolling pin. Place your dough in the middle of the mat and roll it out to a 10-inch circle of even depth. Lift gently and transfer to your tart pan or pie dish, trimming excess dough above the rim and discarding. Repeat the rollout with the second ball of dough, cover your filling, and crimp the edge of the top crust to your bottom with either a fork or by pinching with your fingers. Cut two to three slits in the top and proceed to bake.

Spinach, Bacon, and Wild Rice Frittata

I cook rice often and usually make more than what I need, using the leftovers for other dishes. Such was the case the other night, when my refrigerator was also empty. There wasn't much left beyond a few eggs, some fresh spinach, and a pound of bacon. I was thinking quiche, but didn't want something so egg dense and I was lazy to make a crust. *Hmmm,* I thought to myself, *I wonder if I can whip up a frittata of sorts?* Turns out I could. Here's what you'll need:

INGREDIENTS

2 cups of cooked wild rice
1 pound of bacon, cooked and chopped medium
16 ounces of fresh baby spinach leaves
1 tablespoon of bacon fat or olive oil
4 eggs

½ cup of whole milk
2 tablespoons of melted butter
½ teaspoon of cayenne pepper
Salt and ground black pepper to taste
¾ cup of panko crumbs
½ cup of grated fresh parmesan cheese

INSTRUCTIONS

1. Use leftover wild rice from the night before or whip up two cups in a rice cooker or on the stovetop with a couple tablespoons of butter and chicken stock instead of water (one cup of liquid for every measured cup of rice).

2. Cook your bacon in a 380-degree oven for 17 to 25 minutes on a foil-covered jellyroll pan (page 27–29).

3. While the bacon is cooking, chop your baby spinach finely, but don't mince it.

4. In a large saucier, braising pan, or wide-mouthed sauté pan, heat the bacon fat or olive oil over medium low heat. Add the spinach in batches, stirring until they start to wilt—just enough so each batch is a third reduced in size. Immediately transfer the spinach to a mixing bowl. You're not really trying to cook the spinach here; just reduce its volume and take some water out of it.

5. Rough chop your bacon and add it to the wild rice (if using leftover cold rice, run a fork through to separate the grains).

6. Whisk your eggs with milk, melted butter, cayenne, salt, and pepper. Pour over the spinach, wild rice, and bacon in the mixing bowl and combine with a wooden spoon or rubber spatula. Spread the mixture in a shallow glass pie dish or ceramic tart pan. Neither should require greasing, though you can go ahead and spray it with an all-natural non-stick cooking spray or wipe the pan with olive oil. Even the top out with the spatula and sprinkle with salt and cracked black pepper. Mix the panko and parmesan together and distribute evenly across the top.

7. Set the dish in a 350-degree oven for 30 to 40 minutes. Peek at it toward the 30-minute mark to make sure the panko and parmesan topping isn't browning too much. If the dish is still glistening under the panko, the egg is likely not cooked. If a toothpick stuck in the middle comes out wet, it still needs more time in the oven. If the top is done but you don't think it's cooking through correctly, cover loosely with foil to keep the topping from browning further and go for 10-minute increments until the egg is done.

8. When the frittata is done, set it on a trivet or cold burner and cover with a clean dish towel. Let it sit for five to 10 minutes, then cut into wedges and serve. I slid a nice over-easy fried egg on top of mine for an oversized garnish, and I just loved the runny yolk over this delightfully light meal. Along with a glass of white wine, this makes a wonderful weekend brunch or dinner on a warm summer evening.

Sweet and Spicy Baconated Brussels Sprouts

Brussels sprouts are one of those love 'em or hate 'em type of vegetables. Since you're reading a recipe about them here, you're safe to assume that I fall into the former camp. I love the combination of earthy, dense, cabbagey funk that has a sweetness a cabbage doesn't have.

My favorite way to prepare Brussels sprouts is to wrap each little sprouty nugget in a half-strip of bacon, roasting the batch until the bacon is cooked and the sprouts are fork tender (about 45 minutes to an hour in a 325- to 350-degree oven). One way I like to prepare these is with a drizzle of balsamic vinegar—the real balsamic vinegar here that consists of the necessary ingredient "aged grape must," not the $7, watery el cheapo stuff you find in the grocery store. Another way to play with this vegetable is with this recipe here. You'll need:

INGREDIENTS

1 pound of bacon
15 to 20 Brussels sprouts
1 tablespoon of soy sauce
1 tablespoon of sesame oil

⅓ cup of duck sauce
¼ cup of Chinese hot mustard
1 teaspoon of hot chili flakes (optional)

INSTRUCTIONS

1. Cook your bacon in a 380-degree oven from 17 to 25 minutes on a foil-covered jellyroll pan (page 27–29), but undercook it just a smidge. You want to render out the heaviest of the grease, but you want the slices a little limp, not brown and crispy. Set it aside to drain.

2. While the bacon's cooking, take your Brussels sprouts, cut off the toughest part of the stem end, and halve the whole sprout. You want about four cups to serve as a side in a dinner for four.

3. In a roomy sauté pan, warm up the soy sauce and sesame oil on a medium-high setting, then add in your sprout halves, tossing to coat. Let the pan sit without a cover, occasionally stirring the Brussels sprouts so they don't burn, but allowing them to caramelize and brown.

4. Rough chop your bacon and add to the Brussels sprouts. Lower the flame to medium and stir from time to time until the bacon is done. Add the duck sauce, hot mustard, and red chili flakes, tossing to coat, then lid the pan and lower the flame again. You want enough flame to generate steam within the pan to finish cooking the Brussels sprouts, but not so high that you're continuing to brown. Stir occasionally to distribute the flavors until you can easily skewer the biggest Brussels sprout with a fork. Serve hot with extra crumbled bacon on top.

5. This is an excellent side to chicken, beef, and, of course, pork that is roasted, grilled, or kebabed with a teriyaki marinade. It pairs well next to a beautiful roast that is treated simply with salt and pepper. It's also wonderful served over fluffy jasmine rice if you're looking for an extra carb boost.

Tasso and Spiced Red Lentil Stew

If you haven't been fortunate enough to try tasso before, you're definitely missing something. A peppery and righteously spiced smoked portion of a Boston butt, it's an invention that has its roots in Louisiana. Tasso makes a frequent appearance in dishes of Creole origin, and you might possibly have tasted it if you've had real, honest-to-gawd jambalaya in that state of unique Southern charm.

Tasso is unique in the world of smoked foods. It is the result of a very short salt cure—just hours, not days—followed by a dredging in spices common to Creole cooking and a hot smoke. I have never tasted another smoked meat like it. When sliced, it is dark pink and well-marbled so many people mistake it for ham; but it's not, it's the shoulder, with a gorgeous, dark caramel bark to the outside. Even though I often give suggestions for substitutions in my recipes, this is one recipe in which you should *not* substitute any other meat for the tasso. Its flavor profile is singularly tasso and no other smoked meat, no matter how it was cured, spiced, or smoked, will taste like it. If I don't smoke my own tasso, I get it store-bought from the brand D'Artagnan.

Here's what you'll need for this recipe:

INGREDIENTS

1 cup of finely diced carrots

1 cup of finely died celery (including hearts and leaves)

1 medium sweet onion, diced fine

2 tablespoons of butter

3 tablespoons of minced garlic

2 tablespoons of sweet curry powder

2 tablespoons of vadouvan*

1 tablespoon of tumeric

Salt to taste

3 cups of chicken stock

3 cups of tasso, chopped to fork-sized pieces

1 16-ounce bag of dried red lentils

1 to 3 cup of water

Vadouvan is a pre-blended spice mix, a French take on an Indian curry spice mix that consists of garlic, shallots, curry leaves, cardamom, cayenne, onion, black pepper, cumin, coriander, fenugreek, and turmeric. I got mine at Williams-Sonoma, but a quick Google search shows that it is available from Amazon and other places. Mine is a split-pea soup in color and has a very fine ground. When I open the jar, the aroma immediately transports me to every good Indian restaurant I've ever eaten at. Wonderful, heady stuff, what most would think of as the essence of Indian cooking.

INSTRUCTIONS

1. Mince the carrots, celery, and onion until very fine (I put mine through the food processor for a uniform mince) and add to a stockpot in which you've melted the butter over medium-high heat. Sweat the veggies for 10 or 15 minutes to pull out some of their water, then add the garlic, spices (including vadouvan), and a teaspoon of salt. Stir to combine, then reduce the flame to medium and lid the pot for 10 minutes, stirring occasionally. When it starts to take on a homogenous look, add in stock, tasso, lentils and enough water to cover by an inch.

2. Bring the temperature up a bit. Lentils cook in a flash, unlike dried beans like Navy, Great Northern, Pinto, and kidney beans. Lid the pot to help, but stir frequently and keep an eye on it as the lentils will thicken this from soup to stew before you can blink.

3. When the soup is done, it will be milkshake-with-a-spoon-not-a-straw thick. Despite the cheery orange color of the dried red lentils, this soup will look closer to the color of split peas. Ladle this up piping hot with hot flatbread on the side to swipe the bowl when you're done.

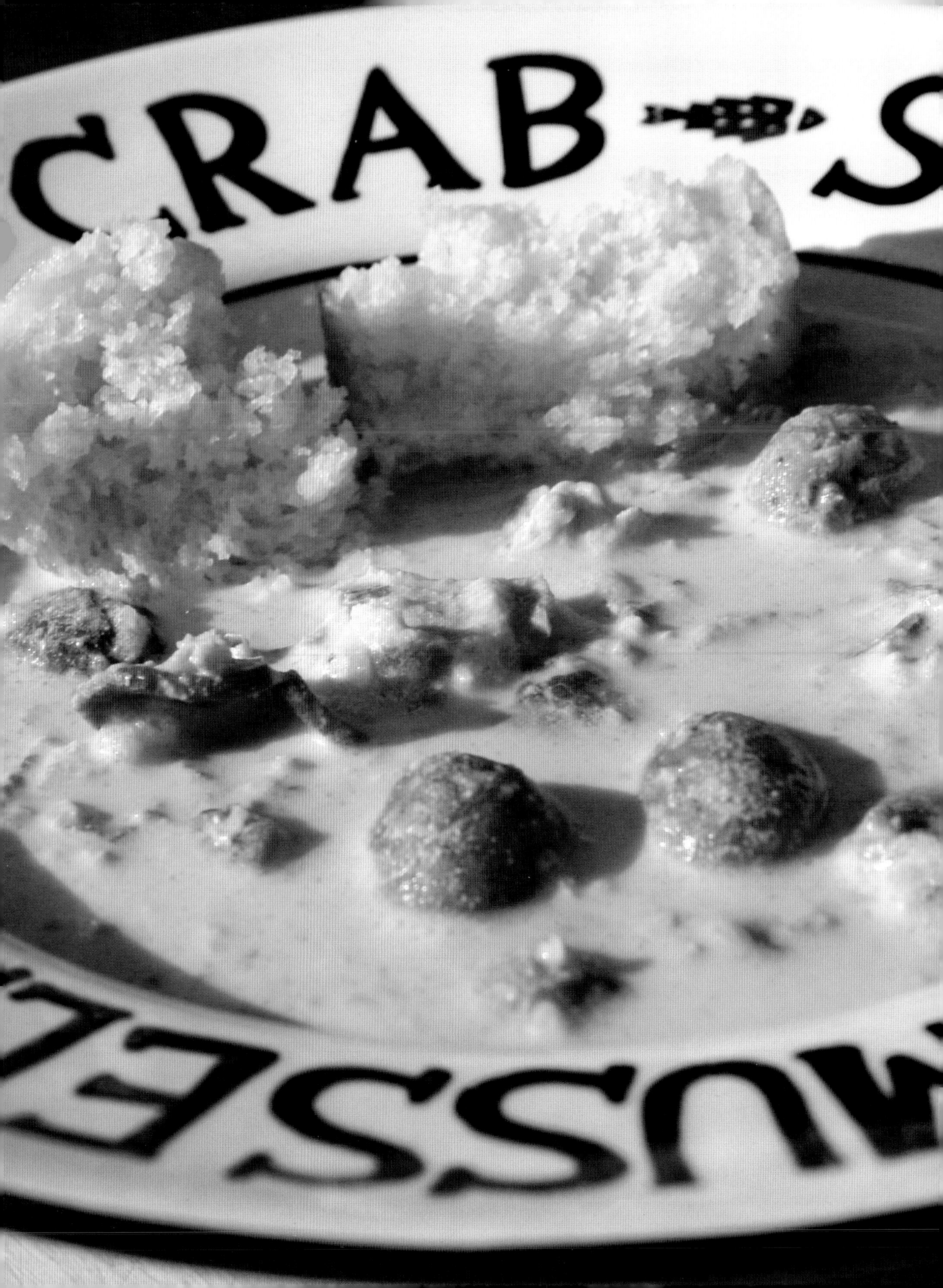
CRAB

Connecticut Clam Chowder

Creamy, rich, New England clam chowder has long been a favorite of mine. To enhance this classic recipe, I thought of a way to work pork into it.

Now, most New England clam chowders use bacon or smoked ham hock in the soup base to add a little fat and flavor. Since bacon is easier to deal with than ham hock, that was the way I went with this recipe. Here's what you'll need:

INGREDIENTS

2 cups of baby potatoes**
Salt and pepper to taste
2 tablespoons of butter
3 tablespoons of garlic
4 cups of fresh chopped clams with its juice*
1 ½ pounds of bacon
3 cups of milk
3 cups of clam stock
2 cups of heavy cream

1 tablespoon Old Bay seasoning
1 tablespoon of garlic powder
1 tablespoon of onion powder
1 ½ cups of finely diced carrots
1 ½ cups of chopped celery
1 large yellow onion
2 tablespoons of bacon fat
Butter and flour for a thickening roux
  if necessary

*TIP My grocer sells clams both in the shell and shucked and minced, which really means a nice chop with generous hunks of clam, in their natural juices. If you do not have a resource for fresh clams, research some high-quality brands of canned clams on Google (poor-quality clams will be tiny and tough). You can get them frozen in their juices, or, if your pockets are deep, mail order fresh clams from a fishmonger on either coast.

**TIP My grocery store carries netted bags of baby potatoes in varieties red, white, and red/white/blue. I love them. They roast up into delectable little bites, and the tri-color batch adds flair to a dish. If you don't have such potatoes available, pick a smooth-skinned, thin-skinned, waxy potato such as a Yukon gold or new red potatoes, and leave the skin on and chop them in one-inch chunks.

1. Start by roasting your potatoes. Spread the baby potatoes in a single layer in a gratin dish or low-sided casserole, drizzle with olive oil, and sprinkle with sea salt. Set in a 365-degree oven for 45 minutes to an hour, until the potatoes are fork tender, with a tiny bit of resistance to the fork. Don't go past this point, as you want them to stay intact when you add them to the soup. Set them aside to cool.

2. While the potatoes are roasting, start your stockpot. Melt three tablespoons of butter over medium low heat and add your chopped garlic. Sauté the garlic low and slow until it turns a light golden brown, stirring frequently to get the color even.

3. When the garlic arrives at the desired color and aroma, add your clams, juice and all. Keep the clams and garlic at a low simmer for half an hour or so.

4. Meanwhile, swap out the finished potatoes in the oven for a tray of bacon. I recommend baking your bacon in a 380-degree oven for 17 to 25 minutes on a foil-covered jellyroll pan (page 27–29). If you have really fatty bacon, pour off the rendered fat halfway through the cooking process, otherwise the bacon tends to boil in its own grease. When the bacon's done, pour off the bacon fat into a vessel and drain the bacon on a plate lined with paper towels. When cool enough to handle, rough chop the bacon and add most of it, but not all, to the clams and garlic.

5. Add the potatoes to the chowder along with the milk, clam juice, heavy cream, and spices. Slowly bring to a gentle simmer, stirring frequently, lid on the pot.

6. Start a *mire poix* with the vegetables. Finely dice the carrots, celery, and onion. I ran all my veggies through the food processor for a uniform dice. The key is to get the dice quite fine, but not turn them to mush.

7. In a large sauté pan or saucier, melt a couple tablespoons of bacon fat over medium to medium-high heat (or use the fresh bacon grease from the batch you just cooked). Add diced vegetables a third at a time, stirring to coat in bacon fat. Sweat the *mire poix* down until the carrots become tender and the onions are translucent, then add the remainder of the chopped bacon. Give the pan a couple more minutes on the heat to soften the bacon, then add all of the pan's contents to the chowder, stirring to mix thoroughly.

8. Gradually bring your chowder to a low and easy boil, stirring as you go. Put the lid on, and stir and check frequently to make sure the spuds and clams aren't sticking to the bottom. Raise the temp slowly until you get the chowder bubbling. Once there, drop the burner to low and leave on simmer for at least an hour before serving. Salt and pepper (and possibly add more Old Bay) to taste.

9. For service, you need nothing more than a large bowl, a generous spoon, and an appetite. The chowder should be pleasantly thick (to thicken it more you can always make a roux from flour and butter and work it into the chowder during the last half-hour of cooking) and loaded with fresh clam flavor. A thick biscuit on the side will help clean the bowl.

TIP I did with this chowder what I do with most of my soups. I built the pot throughout an afternoon, simmering for several hours in the early evening after that first boil with all the ingredients assembled. I then turned off the burner and let the pot sit overnight on the cold stove. I refrigerated the pot in the morning, then reheated for dinner the next night. No one in the food safety and compliance business would ever approve of this method, but not once have I ever sickened anyone or gotten sick myself—even in the summer—and I truly believe flavors in ingredient-rich concoctions like this better complement each other when the dish is allowed to progress in this way.